CW01499593

# Dedication

I dedicate this book to my wife, my daughter, sister and brother.

Also, I dedicate to my friend Ian, who stood by me throughout and my friends who read and fed back comments for me, especially Dawn.

I wish to give immense thanks to DALL-E2 which is part of the OpenAI company. Without the AI, this book would be without illustrations. DALL-E2 allows me to visualise elements of this.

# Contents

# Closed for Repairs

David R Patrick

2

# Introduction.

"The chief function of the body is to carry the brain around."

Thomas A. Edison

My whole life has been substantially about my brain. I was never very sporty and apart from ten pin bowling never very good at any sport.

Although my daughter is very gifted as an artist in all forms, and has real skills in singing, entertaining and dancing, the arts were never for me, no matter how hard I tried.

My brain served me very well throughout my life. Until one day in 2015 it didn't. I first suffered an extreme sustained mania that did not switch off for 2 months no matter how tired or medicated I was.

Then after the mania stopped, so did my brain function. It was like a light that burns so bright, it burns itself out. I could no longer think, talk, or even understand what was going on. I was just an observer to the world seeing but not comprehending.

Little did I know it then but it would be over 6 years before I could fully regain cognitive function and become, well me again, albeit with some small quirky changes.

At the time I wrote this I hadn't been able to express what had happened to me to friends and family and originally that was what this book was for.

When I stopped thinking, I stopped interacting and people didn't know what was going on with me at all.

This book was written in the very last stages of my recovery and I wanted to leave the structure to the way that my brain wanted to express it.

The reason for that was that this was the first time I had the opportunity to fully understand what had happened and what it meant for me. A lot of the realisations came as I actually wrote the book.

The book expresses how I processed what happened and the order of the book how I addressed it. I saw this book as encapsulating this whole period and a way that I could deal with and move on from what happened to me.

I learnt a lot from this and a year later I can honestly say I don't dwell really on the lost time. In many ways this experience changed me and I kind of like the differences it has made.

Please note that the way I have approached this book was just to say what I knew and how I felt and not in any way to filter or change that. Any self-deprecation of my state is purely how I felt about myself and in no way reflects on others. We are all unique.

Also please note that the visualisations are not to say this is what these things look like but more that these reflect the way I felt at that time and they still evoke for me feelings from that time.

# Chapter 1

We always used to say at work that easy writing makes hard reading and vice versa. I wanted the experience to be as honest, real and vibrant as it was to me when it happened and to reflect exactly how I felt at that time. I wrote this a year ago and will only add context where I think it is necessary.

To give you some background this book relates to a complete breakdown I suffered in 2015, which was followed by over 2 months of mania and the 6.5 years of physical recovery from brain damage that followed. For everything that has happened since my recovery I will write another book.

I have tried to leave the book structured as it was written (before the editing phase) as I felt it made sense at the time. It was a voyage of discovery for me and a very positive one at that. It does not start at the beginning but towards the end as I explore what has happened. Please stick with me and trust me it will all make sense by the final paragraphs.

Whilst this by necessity talks about me, in the background to everything I did, my wife was running around, sometimes making herself ill, just to keep things going. I struggle to express how grateful I am and mere words don't cover it.

You may think that this experience when you have read it has left me jaded in some way. Strangely it's the opposite. A friend of the family asked how I had changed. It was the last question I was expecting. I wasn't in any of this looking for change, just to get back to where I was before.

Anyway, the answer to the question is that it has given me an infinite regard for the ability of the body to regenerate, of the mind to reform itself. It has also given me an increased sense of wonder how this all (the mind) works and an appreciation of every single day I have being me.

One other thing, which again came up many times in conversations, is how I feel about what happened. For my wife, fully cognizant during all of this, everything still cuts very deep. I find my own answer to this strange but true.

I found myself for a lot of it detached from what was happening to me, firstly forcibly (I wasn't really a part of 2016/2017) and then I think emotionally (to dwell on it would have been too terrible). I remember vividly the fear of doing things because I knew I couldn't do them anymore but that's about it.

When I finally started connecting brain cells through repetitive tasks, strangely I wasn't frustrated like I would be now doing those tasks. I literally couldn't do anything else and it seemed like something to do (at first) just to make my mind work a little. Also, I lacked the capacity for boredom at the time.

As things accelerated, I become enamoured with the brain and how I was changing. A bit like emerging from a cocoon at 1 mm a day (though I am still cocoon shaped).

I never really got angry or felt hard done by because strangely it didn't seem well relevant. I will say I think more than anything this was pure damn luck and something I never thought of at the time.

I hate to think what this time would feel like when sentient and angry all the time or frustrated would be like, that would have seemed a lot longer and believe me the years felt like a long time already.

In regards to Mental Health Services, I have that feeling you have where you don't want these people in your life anymore. In my experience Mental health disorders are often treated like diseases for which medications are the be all and end all, just take your medications and stay quiet, regardless of what it does to you, whether it is helping you or whether you need them.

I have become very aware that what God gives so he can take away… I am very conscious of the blessing of being back to myself and I do not take that for granted. There is a very small chance that whatever gifts I have been granted are temporary.

If that is the case, I have no regrets. To spend one day with my family and friends as the real me virtually or not is more than I could have hoped for in those years. I will be grateful for ever for it. It is not about the duration; it is about the experience. If this is temporary, just let this book sing as to who I really am.

Knowing that people know I am there somewhere if I am not physically "there" is a big part of this for me, as is them knowing during all this time I was gone that I still cared. Honestly, I am surprisingly at peace with this.

I really am not aiming at being melodramatic or narcissistic just honest about my situation. It is what it is. I only include what may be seen as an over sentimental assessment for completeness. It's not like I think it's the likely outcome. Just covering the bases.

Those 6.5 years must have changed me a bit. I have also become more philosophical about things. I couldn't magic my way out of them, so maybe I have learnt acceptance of whatever fate brings. I don't know as it's the first time I am thinking about it but it feels about right.

I have realised in conversations now with several friends and family, especially amongst those I haven't spoken to in a while, a slight hesitance. Do not get me wrong everyone has been fully supportive and everything said is really all as positive as you would expect.

However, underneath the surface I can sense a niggle. A kind of I want to believe you but really. I am in no way blaming people for that. I am a bit of a sceptic myself as anyone that knows me will tell you. The idea that someone goes from reasonably smart to a vegetable, sounds a little ridiculous even to me. And 6.5 years, really?

Unfortunately, I have the cards I am dealt. By being the same person, they knew, did I ever really go away? Maybe people think I just hid away in shame for a while. I could believe that if it wasn't me involved. I may have miscalculated when trying to explain this to people.

By not exposing myself (figuratively) it looks like Dave was fine, Dave had a mental breakdown, Dave disappears and Dave is now fine again. Even I could potentially buy into that.

However, ask my wife, my sister and my daughter (especially my daughter and no of course I don't want you bothering her, leave her alone). They had to deal with the fallout of what I became. From a personal experience as someone that is reasonably smart, I am not sure how I could have pulled of the vegetable act for more than a day without getting extremely bored.

Sorry, this made me laugh. I just imagined who would spend 2.5 years eating cold baked beans and sausages out of a can, to get round an apology. They were delicious mind. I now have a taste for cold canned food. So maybe someone would do it.

Anyway, I am not saying that they are not fully supportive. They all are. That they struggle with the concept is completely natural. It's a lesson for me. I created the dots that they joined. Whilst I did it for my own reasons (didn't have the cognitive power to think about theirs as well) I didn't take account of the experience to them.

You will notice there is a long lead up to the key facts in this as I make various clarifications…. So much is context. To me what is important is where I ended up and it's like I need to explain that first.

# Chapter 2

I want to be clear before I start that this reflects my own experience with anti-psychotic medications and my circumstances. I know for many people that they are a godsend and the very fabric of staying connected to reality.

Once I was diagnosed all the doctors I saw since wanted to do was to leave me on these drugs forever. They didn't care about the side effects or that these drugs, taken when you get older actually can significantly increase your chance of death (I was on one of those).

The doctors literally just seemed to look at the fact that medication meant that the chances of the episode reoccurring reduced from their perspective. The fact it messed with my life had no priority against that or the fact I had only ever had one major event.

I realised in ongoing discussions it was clear that this would never change and that the longer I stayed on the drugs, the more doctors would say this was the reason I had no more episodes, rather than this was an isolated episode in my life.

If I had known what the mental health services would do, I would have stated, that I only wanted to be treated for the period that I am legally required to be after the illness terminated.

These drugs obviously work extremely well for many people that have repeated issues without them, though they can have horrible, life changing side effects. However, for me who had one extended episode in my life I realised once on the conveyor belt with medication there was no off ramp

For me, 2.5 years of abilify was devastation. I forever lost my career, lost all my life-long friendships and caused havoc on those around me by being a walking store dummy.

My sister is a fighter and has as far back as I remember been the same. In the early abilify years I couldn't think or write for myself at all. My sister did that for me.

I recently found a letter that my sister wrote to the DWP in support of an application for ESA for me. The below is a direct extract from that letter and will perhaps give some insight into how I was,

Prior to July 2015;

"He was the most intelligent person I knew and could easily learn new skills."

And how I had become;

"He is now a shadow of the man he was. Gone is the vibrant man that wore you out just listening to him talk

A typical example of David's condition and his inability to complete simple tasks is evidenced by his claim for ESA. I advised David to make a claim for ESA May 2016 and gave him the number to make the claim. I reminded him to call fortnightly — he didn't. I downloaded the form for him to fill in - he didn't.

In December 2016 (7 months later) I ended up filling in the form with him.

When I asked him why he hadn't filled it in - he didn't know- he hadn't even looked at the questions. When I asked why he hadn't asked for help — he didn't know.

It was only recently when I asked him what medical evidence he had sent in — and he looked at me blankly — that I discovered he had not asked any professional to provide information about his mental health."

I couldn't make decisions and when it came to terminating the use of abilify, not being able to vocally defend this with doctors meant I prevaricated on every decision for months. From the snippets I remember and what I have been told I couldn't really understand what was happening.

My sister continually pushed me to make decisions over a period of years. I am thankful she did as I don't think I would have had any form of recovery until I stopped the medication. My sister took me out to dinner, every couple of weeks I think (its blurry especially 2016/2017). Who wants a dinner with an eating automaton? No-one but she did again and again.

I wouldn't categorise the support from my sister as emotional support. That's not really what was needed. Instead, it was a slow but constant push to act, to see what I was ready to take on. Without my sister I do not know where I would have been and I am lucky she chose to take me on.

My sister has continually made meals for us to have at home to help my wife, through this, as well as many other things. This again is a blur in the early years. I know it happened but not what. I know my sister tried to provide emotional support to my wife but I can't say I took in what happened as it doesn't come back.

# Chapter 3

I discovered a few weeks ago I could write creatively again (not that I am making this stuff up, more that it's not a guidebook for a dishwasher). I thought I never would again.

My sister encouraged me to think of others going through the same or similar situation regarding recovery from brain damage and to write something that may help. I found it helped a lot with friends and family and decided to publish to allow people interested in the experience to understand what happened to me, from my perspective.

I realised I hadn't told anyone almost any of what is written in this book because I couldn't communicate, either because I was not of sound mind at the time of the event or because of how damaged my brain was afterwards, so this aims to summarise everything I know about those years.

The reason I am writing now and not earlier. I only started feeling that I recognised myself in any regards (my humour, my belief system, my reasoning, my likes) circa 4.5 years after the event and was only able to express myself verbally in a coherent way maybe in the last year, which I have been constantly experimenting with.

I now feel I can finally express myself adequately in words. Regarding the medication, I have no doubt it stopped me from starting the process of them.

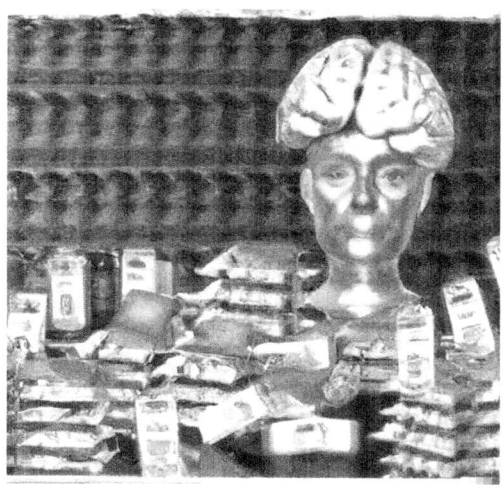

No one in the mental health community listened to me on that, despite me apparently raising the fact I couldn't think every time I received an injection for 2 years.

After all these years somehow, in the last few weeks, I woke up and I just knew that I was myself again. My thinking was completely aligned with who I used to be and how I used to think.

I have no clue how I could possibly know that. Mostly I have focused on cognitive skills recovery but I am as sure as I am that Donald Trump wears fake tan. I can feel it but don't know how. I only include it as I find it fascinating. literally I am me again, in all senses I can judge.

It's weird, I use the pre industrial sleep method (that people used through history until industrialisation). It's simple. Sleep for a few hours, get up do stuff for a couple of hours then have a longer second sleep. I am not working (haven't since this happened in 2015) and for some reason it suits me.

I have also had a realisation, that maybe that is why my wife struggles to discuss this. If this is temporary, she and my daughter will have had to go through a false dawn, only to be dumped back in the same place we were before.

This incident just happened. Our washing machine broke down and my wife called me in to help. I tried to deal with the problem but saw my wife get upset. I didn't understand why.

She said that where I used to be commanding at work, I was always much more sensitive with her and empathetic. I apparently had been more assertive like I was with work colleagues for the first time, which they will tell you is not sensitive! I didn't realise I had done that.

Shit, this is not going to be the walk in the park I was hoping for. I hadn't really thought through the ramifications of recovering, just laboured towards it. Like digging a tunnel, I guess only worrying where it will come out after completing it.

I have obviously changed in some key ways, without even knowing it had happened. The last person I want to treat badly is my wife. OK so this recovery is not all a rose garden.

This prompted a conversation that has been too hurtful for my wife to have. She told me she always believed I would find a way through. I feel honoured she could have thought that about me. After all I couldn't boil a kettle. How can someone have such faith. She is my hero.

By necessity me and my wife broached my period of mental illness several years before, which we had never discussed since. Just the mention of my manic period was enough for my wife to cry. She has gone through so much more than I did. I realise now that I got away lightly in this. How is that fair on her?

Wow things are getting a more complicated but hey I dealt with complicated before. Fingers crossed I can get through this.

# Chapter 4

When I came "back" I re-established connections with friends. I had cut ties with virtually everyone when the extent of the damage to my cognitive thinking became clear.

The only significant interactions of any form I had for a number of years were at home with my wife and daughter, when my sister took me out for dinner every couple of weeks and when once a week the one friend I stayed in contact with, sat with me in a pub.

At the time myself and my family thought it was only medication causing the issue, my family thought I would be in contact with them in 6, 12, 18 months.  That timeline slipped away further to the distance, as my future on abilify stopped having an end date.

When I finally got off the medications and I was still exactly the same, we then had to face that I may be like that forever.

In the early years there wasn't much communication associated with any of those interactions. Even as I started recovery, I didn't mix with anyone outside my family apart from the one friend really until the last year or so (so over 5 years) and that was limited.  This included calling people on the phone which I have only started doing recently.

It was the first time I had contacted them in several years.  Being alone in my world as it existed, was not the same ongoing pain and reminders of a life I once knew than if I had maintained contact.  To be plain, I couldn't take on the extra pain of being a vegetable, mixing with clever and articulate people and I didn't want them to see me like that anyway.

I didn't want to get back in touch with people until I knew I was me in all significant regards and with a vocabulary that I could express myself properly to apologise for what happened and to explain why I lost contact. It's a little weird as people pick up and we are interacting as if nothing has happened.

I had been fully prepared to never speak to my friends again, if I hadn't recovered.

Not because I don't treasure them, I do but I didn't want to contact them as a shell of my former self. Some may call that vanity, it wasn't. Maybe a little deference to who I used to be. Not that I was all that but I was happy in my Family Guy sized skin.

Initially I only contacted a small number of friends based on the set of friends I was friendly with when I had my breakdown. As I am in these final stages of recovery my brain is screaming for interaction (I can literally feel it) and I asked my friends for two things.

One to read this book as it stood at the time, to understand what happened to me before we talked about it. The second to call me afterwards just to talk to help with the final stages of recovery.

From my own side, I was actually nervous and worried it may be overload for me. This may sound strange but it feels like it's not me that needs these phone calls and the interaction it's my brain. I have been in a vacuum for so long, I think it natural that when the brain finally lets itself loose it wants to get to its optimum quickly.

I know, I know I am not a brain surgeon or anything but me and my brain have been alone together for some time. I am starting to get an inkling as to what it does and what it wants.

People really took their time to read the book. Perfectly understandable as they all have busy lives but left me a little bemused as I would have found a way to read as much as I could the first night.

I am not saying I am right it is just what I would do. Honestly it is. Even if I had to stay up all night to accommodate that I would. In my world friendship means laying yourself on the line and making sacrifices so that the one in need doesn't hurt.

I thought that's what everyone believed. What I have come to realise both in the request for reading the book and the request to be able to just chat, is how much friendship changes to many people with time.

Everyone was just too busy to actually do anything. It's understandable if that's the way you think; if day to day things take priority. It just is what it is. All of my friends were older, most had families and they took priority.

One friend however has shone. He has a busier life than everyone else with many kids and a very demanding job. He somehow found the time every single day to make time for me at the expense of things he wanted to do. I can't criticize anyone. My definition of friendship is different to theirs. Except for this friend.

Actually, how could I have forgot my dad's friend that is now my friend. He has quietly been there all through this experience. We had been friendly for decades but started being friends around the time my dad died the year before my breakdown. He visited me every other day in the mental health hospital, he has never ever judged me or threw back in my face all the things he must have seen. He has just got on with it.

He sat with me every week, in the pub for 6 years. Wow. How bad am I that he didn't jump to mind? So, he knows what I mean about what it means to be a friend. It's just different to people where being a friend means being only doing things where anything needed can fit around TV, work, shopping, eating, mowing the lawn and other commitments.

He never ever said a word about any of it, he was just always there. I hope I can be as much of a friend to him as he was to me.

For three of the six friends I called, they said they would call, they did once and that was it. All were just too busy. At first, I thought maybe they had been kidnapped. It made me realise just how much priorities change and for some how friendships fade against that. It actually helped me to know.

I had never asked anyone for anything before this situation, looking back I was too proud. When this stage occurred and I needed to talk, it was not something I wanted, it was something I needed.

It is just what it is. For me I am glad I know. My favourite quote of all time is "We see the world not as it is, but as we are".

How perfect is that and how well does it reflect the differences between people.

I told my friends from the above exactly what I was thinking, which was a mistake. My wife told me in no uncertain terms to back off and let people deal with things in their own way.

I have backed off. I don't mess with my wife when she tells me something. Ever. I really mean Ever. She can be fierce and she knows how to put me in my place and fast.

Now this bit makes me laugh, a lot. I have an acerbic sense of humour; I always have but it mellowed after the birth of my daughter My daughter. All of the friends I have recontacted have told me my humour has changed from when we lost contact in 2015.

I hadn't noticed but to be honest with so much going on I miss things like this. Apparently, people told me my humour was more like the year 2000 (I have known these guys for decades, A sure sign of being old).

Now they say it, I can feel it. I know right. That is kind of lame but it's true. Why on earth would my mind reset to an earlier sense of humour. I am afraid I have absolutely no idea. I will wait and see whether someone with a bigger brain than me can tell me.

I find myself awake at 4am and wanting to talk. My brother in New Zealand is obviously doing stuff and my mate in the US, well I have no idea. We were sending funny messages all day but he is obviously busy with something. So here I am back with you.

It's strange how kind of needy for social contact I have become. That isn't quite right not needy but craving for social interaction of any sort. I guess it's my brain saying please feed me. I should state, I now have a group of ½ dozen long term friends I am in regular contact with and that I am more than happy with.

# Chapter 5

As I was saying before I am not carrying the past with me. I am thankful for whatever time I have now back as me. Many people never get that and I know it's a blessing.

All that hurts me now is the pain this has caused to my wife, daughter and sister. I feel guilty telling my story, when my family suffered so much. I am now through this but like PTSD, this illness still ravages other members of my family.

My wife told me the other day, which I thought was for the first time, about someone else that had brain damage at her school and that it took several years to come back and she only managed it through retraining her brain. Apparently, she told me many times over the years. It's a real shame it never permeated as that was pure gold.

Another thing I have only just become aware of. To give context I am a fat man. So, fat at the moment you could take an average adult male of fat out of me and I would not be underweight. I have put over 100lb of weight on since lockdown and I hate to think how much of that was since I turned into a vegetable.

Since I have come out of hospital a week ago, I have not been hungry except for a meal a day, which in itself is a delightful diabetic meal (not). I have lost maybe 10kg, without any thought. I haven't tried I just haven't been hungry. I have been working on this book every day and I get lost sometimes in it.

I am now delicately asking questions of my wife about what I was like before 2015 on specific things. This is because although my memories have come back some things like how much I ate, I can't remember.

For example, I was really surprised that since coming out from hospital and especially when writing this book, I was only eating one meal a day and wondered if I had ever done that before. My wife said often when I worked and was in the middle of a project that was particularly challenging, I only ate one meal a day. I can't for the life of me remember that.

Isn't the brain just a fascinating organ. How the hell does it keep slipping these things past me. I thought I was clever and my brain was an organ. The fact that physically the brain is capable of this recovery is a marvel I will never forget.

With the book I can see some parallels with what used to be my work, which essentially was about solving corporate puzzles, which I got deeply involved in. Whilst writing the book I was so interested in it that I didn't notice I wasn't eating. I guess that must have been the same with work.

I always used to say, I am nothing without my brain and to lose that in any regard, would be to lose me as a person. That is exactly how I felt, when I could start to rationalise it, that I had lost myself. That was one of the saddest aspects for me.

I do however feel in all of this that somehow my brain protected me from the worst of it. I have never been someone who suffered from depression.

However, looking back on this I find it interesting that I didn't get bouts of depression during this and that surprises me. I had the feelings of inadequacy at key moments, for years when I dwelled on it and I felt I would never be myself again, yet I didn't get depressed and I moved on each time.

I hope one day my daughter sees this book. I want to give her context to what happened to me and how I am really ok. She saw me have a meltdown on the doorstep where I just couldn't cope and couldn't support my wife through her period of loss of both parents in the few days, I was home between hospital stays.

Subsequently her father being away afterwards first literally as I went back to hospital for several weeks, figuratively as the person who returned was a shell. My body may have been left but I wasn't there. That has stuck like a knife with me as I loved being a father with all my heart and to lose that, well that is sad.

After my father died myself, my brother and my sister realised that we didn't have anywhere with his voice captured. Whatever else happens if anyone needs to be with me, they can spend a couple of hours here and they can always hear my voice.

In my comparisons to a vegetative state, I do not underestimate the plights of others that truly live through indignity. It is purely a way of me expressing just how empty and non-functional I was. I was often described even by family as a shell.

I am surprised as I write this, how little of it I have discussed with anyone for all sorts of reasons. It makes you realise that in these situations the clues you give to the outside world can be very limited and you limit them further by suppressing information.

For many years my family wouldn't have had any clues what was going on with me at all as initially I couldn't communicate. After that as my ability to comprehend and form basic communication with my family developed, I didn't want to worry others and I didn't want people to despair.

You worry that information about how bad things still were after years without any kind of way forward would only make people feel worse. Additionally, for so long I worried if I would even be able to express myself properly.

It's strange but I guess even though that information may have somehow helped, I remember an absolute reluctance to share information as I knew as our situation was desperate and I had caused enough carnage, to not provide false hope in my messages.

An example was when I stopped taking anti-psychotics. There were two schools of thought. One involved a very slow graduation of coming off the drugs over a period of a year or so. The other one-month ½ dose, then the next month nothing.

I did the latter but said to my family I was taking the slow path. This gave me a significant amount of time to see whether my mental facilities would improve. They didn't after I completely quit although my general slow path to recovery started soon after. Looking back, I can see it wasn't that long after I started logging on to the PC and started doing the very basic things.

I hadn't told anyone about me maybe not recovering as, well some subjects are too difficult to discuss if you think things will stay that way forever. To go down that path is to acknowledge your life's lot and for me and from my family's perspective that may have been too difficult to bear.

In this case as my family believed I was coming off the medication very slowly towards the end of the time, they realised I wasn't changing and that changes may be for the long term.

I will only touch on this but the additional financial pressures of me not working throughout this also, as you can imagine, had a significant impact and changes the way you live.  This isn't the determining factor in anything but the loss of my income had a big impact, it taints everything as money affects the fundamentals of our existence and that just worsens the overall experience.

Even now this is so difficult to openly talk about as my wife has coped, effectively on her own, whilst working, raising a daughter and dealing with a vegetable for many years, with no one to talk to about it.  She has had to suppress and hold down her own fears and concerns.  To talk about it cuts very deep, very quick.

It's not fair on her.  I wish I had a way of magically taking that pain on myself but I can't and I hate that.  I would never have had the opportunity to come back without her full support.

# Chapter 6

Though I may find out in the future, there are still things I don't know about during those first few years after the brain damage. It's very difficult to raise certain subjects as they become triggers for the whole thing with my wife. Just touching the subject of those years, triggers reactions I don't want to invoke.

What I know is that I showed no signs at all of recovery and throughout struggled to express a meaningful sentence of any kind.

I couldn't cook and couldn't really understand instructions so ate food directly out of tins when my wife was as work.

I have been a little excitable about getting my brain back and I have realised that others, are only so flexible about it. Of course, they are, they have their lives to lead. Some things that make me laugh. No one had said until yesterday that my messages were pinging during the day or overnight.

I know this is ridiculous but that hadn't crossed my mind. I use do not disturb, so I don't get pings overnight and I use notification silencing on WhatsApp. So, it didn't happen to me. The thing is and sorry I am chuckling but I have regained my typing speed (I am pretty damn nifty on a computer keyboard) and I use WhatsApp on the desktop most of the time.

So, I have been sending messages since reconnecting at all hours to everyone. More than that I type relatively short sentences on

WhatsApp so they get the message quick in normal conversation. For each message someone sends me I often send 10-12.

Again, a chuckle. So, I have been sending dozens of pings at a time and sometimes 100 in a day, to people overnight and while they are at work without realising. People didn't say anything for 4 days. I guess they were giving me space. Anyway, it's not funny really but I cannot fully suppress the laugh.

So many strange as in odd things happened as part of this 6.5-year period. Lots of little things but for me I wonder, just wonder why. As an example, I always used to drink coffee.

Way too much sometimes as many as 20 cups a day up until 2015. When a day until I suffered the gallstones situation and was hospitalised (very recent).

There was that sudden lifting of the veil that bought me back to a person I recognised. Since that point all, I can think about is tea, I am drinking 7 cups a day. In my life I don't remember drinking tea in any significant regard but I have zero interest in coffee anymore and absolutely love tea.

I have no idea what happened but I am convinced it is something to do with my cognitive development.

# Chapter 7

Its probably the right time to start the discussion about what happened and the timelines for it.

I was 51 when my mental health deteriorated for the first time, in my life. The mental health condition I experienced was an extended period of maybe 10-11 weeks in which I had a continuous mania which didn't abate even while medicated by anti-psychotics.

This was except for a period in which I was given Zombie pills (that's what the patients called them) that left me drooling and not knowing where or who I was.

It was pretty frightening for me and for those I know and love that surrounded me. During this period, I was truly not myself.

I knew what was happening to me in snippets and bits but my thought processes, well I look back and it's like I was an observer and I only got to tune in now and again. Vast swathes I don't remember.

I knew something was happening to me though and things were wrong at distinct points for example I rang several mental health charities before the situation escalated and talked to at least 3 people in those charities for an initial consult.

After I was first released from hospital. I had not fully recovered; in fact, I was a long way from it as was shown by me being there another several weeks upon re-entry. The only reason I had been let go was that my wife and daughter had returned from Japan.

I asked to be taken back after a few days as I couldn't cope and had to persuade the Accident and Emergency people over several hours to allow me to go back to the assessment centre for admission.

Being released early caused 2 long lasting effects. One, rather than being treated as a single time period that I was ill, the second time I was admitted to hospital a few days later it was treated as though it was a completely different incident and that is treated as an ongoing issue rather than an isolated event.

Ongoing issue in my case meant that they determined this was a problem for life. This is a curse I haven't yet been able to get rid of, as no matter how long since I was ill, as far as the Mental Health Services are concerned, I am on remission.

I was extremely unwell in that period and the second effect was that my wife and daughter saw me when I was in a very bad way between hospital stays and that was truly awful.

I will later write about what happened, as I know it, in detail. In mental health situations you are generally diagnosed whilst in their care.

I understand that people need to have a diagnosis and in the absence of other information doctors settle on what is presented. The fact that this was never revisited or that the initial concerns raised by doctors about investigation of physical health were never followed up is however a problem to me.

Having never had mania before, the experience was unlike anything else I knew, ever. I felt a clarity of thought I had never had which in initial stages meant I got an incredible amount of work done but later this clarity warped from reality. I believe it was in this period that damage to my brain occurred. For over 2 months the mania was constant and I felt like my brain was on fire.

By the stage this had stopped so had my cognitive function, which was attributed to the anti-psychotics at the time, as being the only thing that was different other than having had a manic attack. It was also the only medication I was taking.

That was the start of my real, physical recovery as my brain function never came back on its own, even after stopping all medication after years.

I will say that there are extended periods where my ability to recollect timelines doesn't exist at all, especially during the first few years after mania during the time I was taking anti-psychotics. I tend to have to put memories in blocks of time. I also can't recollect everything, it's like the memories at the time were also affected.

In fact, late 2015 (last 3 months), I remember nothing at all, 2016/2017 there was a small block of 5 or 6 weeks where somehow, I managed to attend (though not achieve) work.

However, I only managed to secure the job because of my past reputation and even in that short period I was apparently signed off sick for a significant part, with stress (I found the sick note recently). From what I have been told, I struggled the entire time because I couldn't think properly. Most of 2016/2017 is a blank (although I have odd recollections during those 2 years).

2018 is when I came of abilify and that's where my memories start really in a way I could put in a timeline. I have been told by my sister it is isn't a bad thing that I can't remember those first years. Now I am past it, strangely I wish I could as I have lost the ability to trace improvement or the lack of it in many things.  Saying that I can't and my family couldn't recall any improvements at all until I stopped abilify.

However strangely I do remember a lot of specific things and things I didn't process at the time, I can now.  As time has gone on and my brain function has increased my memory of some of the specific times has got better.

What was interesting to me was how long it took me to recognise the person I am now as fundamentally the person I was before.  This to me was one of the scariest things as I worried constantly whether I was the same person and if not the me from before, who was I now.

I think it was about 4 ½ years before I recognised myself again and knew I was fundamentally the same person from before with the same underlying beliefs and the same likes and dislikes.

I have been outgoing and determined as far back as I remember until I was ill in 2015.  Following that I lost cognitive function (more later). That experience reset my character and I became insular, scared and withdrawn.  The reason for this was because I knew I couldn't do anything mentally.  I couldn't look after myself in the way I had before.

What I mean by this is that we all have our natural defences and actions.  We know our own mind, our arguments, can state our positions etc. I couldn't. In the absence of that I felt leaving the house was dangerous to me.

To show how long lasting this concern was, I had a twelve-week course that finished maybe just under 5 years into recovery with a psychiatrist about talking to people.

At that stage I couldn't talk to anyone other than my family and one friend. I find that difficult now to imagine myself in that position, knowing myself before 2015 and as of now.

It is interesting to me to read what I wrote during that 12-week course. I wrote that I was an embarrassment to my former self and by interacting with people I was letting that person who used to exist down by denigrating his image (I didn't use those exact words! I didn't have them).

This wasn't to anyone else; it was to me as part of an exercise I had to do. A letter from the past you may say. This may seem stupid to some but put me in that same position and I would think and do the same thing again.

I worried that people would wonder what had gone wrong with me and feel sorry for me, which was the last thing I wanted. It's weird I wanted to protect the image of the person I used to be even at the expense of myself at the time because I didn't see myself at that time as worth anything.

It's strange really, my only development in relation to engagement and interaction since that course is the several months in 2020/2021 where I worked 2 mornings a week in a charity shop, though that experience helped me a lot. It forced me to interact and to talk to people and to exchange information. This was very significant for me.

I think the key here, is that by this stage my basic cognitive skills were developing and the way to repair my brain established, I could do this. There is no way I would have been able to deal with the outside world until I had basic cognitive function and I don't believe I would have developed at work; without this rigour I had developed and the skills I had already attained.

One little thing about that experience, when I first went to the charity shop, the manager had a son with extreme challenges. She dealt with me, nicely mind, as I imagine she did with her son. I was initially put in the back room to work on things.

Only over time was I exposed to customers. I was scared silly of using the cash till machine when several months in I was assigned to it. Something so basic and fundamental yet to me it was one of the biggest challenges I had faced in that 6.5 years.

It's difficult but I still feel the uncertainty I had as to whether I could process the till when I recall that. The truth was I forgot many times on how to do it. Almost every 80-year-old there was more adroit and adept at handling it. I am so thankful for how patient they were with me.

# Chapter 8

I always used to be able to have several WhatsApp chats on the go before my breakdown and I wrote a lot more than each of the people I was talking to.

I found that as I wrote very fast, I could type a lot quicker and raise issues in messages quicker than in general conversation and so I could have many conversations at one time. I suppose it's my version of that thing people do when they have several chess matches on the go. I suddenly have that again (last few days).

What surprised me is my typing speed has returned, to the point that I cannot tell the difference to how it was at its peak. I have been trying to think when this happened and I cannot place it. However conversely since my world for the last few years has been so small, I probably didn't need the speed.

It's a very strange thing. I had no intention about writing about this sort of stuff. I just kind of feel it's part of the whole recovery thing, adjusting back to normality. It's a strange ride this final piece. Things that were normal before I was ill in 2015 now to family seem abnormal.

I find myself sitting ready for anyone to respond. However, I used to have 1 contact I exchanged regular chats with post 2015 (family doesn't count as you tend to talk instead). Now I have 11. Not the hundreds I used to have. So, I am aware I am just waiting most of the time as normal people get on with their lives.

After spending time anxiously waiting for someone to message me so I could have a chat, I re-evaluated. After many years of only talking to one person outside my immediate family maybe twice a week, I had re-established contact with close friends. To be fair I thought that may overload me. In fact, it has proved to be the opposite.

As people are busy, I realised I needed much more engagement and I reopened doors with other friends, including those with ever more difficult explanations I needed to give about my actions of 2015. Again, I am just blown away how much smarter with this stuff my brain is than I am.

I wasn't ready I thought and was quite worried about talking to people again. However suddenly I had deep, rich conversations again, some lasting for hours. Something I hadn't done for many years. My brain knew I was ready, it just had to push me into doing it.

I also decided, now that I could explain, I had to make right with everyone I had wronged in 2015 and began the process of connecting with people to explain, including all those I had wronged. Having this book has helped so much in that process.

I have to say people were so kind about what had happened. Again, I think having all the information about it helped.

Up until recently, I just didn't feel I had the tools to explain and then there was so much context I wanted to give about what was happening. I realised that I would never achieve that verbally.

There is so much here, I couldn't explain it all in other ways. So, thanks book. It's the sort of thing I wish I had realised. Its only luck that it exists and that I am able to do it.

It's weird I stopped writing for a bit. Not because I haven't been enjoying it by the way. I have been loving it but because of the thrill of having conversations once more. I need to balance as what happens out there allows me to complete the journey in here.

I don't know whether people realise that the degree of interaction I have with them is determining the pace of change and recovery in me. The brain is so fascinating. Who would have thought that my brain was doing so much in the background bringing me back?

I have also discovered swearing has slipped back into my language. Not in your average situation but if someone is doing something silly (tried to tone that down) and obviously not in front of family. I only ever used to swear at work. Still trying to wrap my head round that one.

If you don't know me by the end of this book, I am afraid my friend you never will. I apologize that it jumps a bit between light and dark. However, that is my experience. All the later (in time) stuff, well mostly is light. The earlier stuff not so much.

# Chapter 9

I bite my nails like badly. I have done since I was a child and I know it's an awful habit. I realised recently I hadn't bitten my nails. What's strange is I only noticed when they got in the way. It must have been at least 4 weeks growth

Now I know you are going to want an explanation but here is the thing. I want to understand why as well. What on earth caused me to suddenly stop a lifetime of biting nails, without even realizing. You must admit... This brain thing is fascinating.

A number of people who read early versions of this book described the style as like a fireside chat. I like that a lot. Since a lot of what I write is the first time I have addressed that particular area, I found I wanted someone with me (in a virtual way), to go through it with.

It was like I didn't want to face it alone as I wasn't sure of my reaction facing these things. I found it very comforting and my approach was to make that person, you the reader. I have never done anything like that before though I may with another book.

If you want more fireside chats by the way just search for me, the next book won't be long after this one. That is if I haven't bored you by now.

Finally on this element my daughter has grown up in a house full of frightening change. First, she saw me between the first and second hospitalisation (she was in Japan for the leadup to the first) and she saw me have a meltdown. God how bad that was but honestly, I couldn't cope at that point and had no self-control.

It was particularly sad as my wife was talking about the loss of her mum and the imminent loss of her father (which was the reason that my wife and daughter were in Japan).

All my life I have been empathetic. At work and in my private life. I was always someone that people turned to when life went bad for them. However, at this point, I was in a really bad place mentally, and should have been in hospital (I would be within a few days). I still knew I needed to support my wife but couldn't get my mind to function properly to do this and this just it seems led to my meltdown.

Because of what happened to me and how difficult it is for my wife to talk about this period, at the moment we still haven't been able to broach the subject.

My daughter and her mum are so intrinsically linked. Since she was a baby, my daughter can detect the slightest change in temperament or stress in my wife. Its uncanny. However, when my wife is in distress it immediately also touches my daughter.

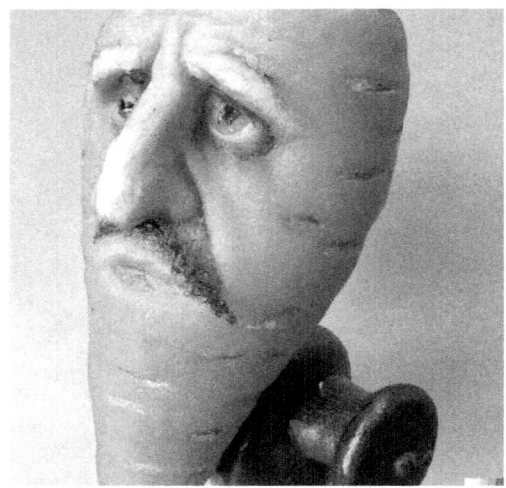

I wish I had that sort of bond but how close can you get to a carrot. We used to be really close. Yes, we were, I can see and feel those memories. Those bonds are lost somewhat, we only hug now a couple of times a year. We used to hug non-stop. My wife and my daughter hug all the time. I am not jealous just maybe a little sad.

I won't stop trying to rebuild the bonds however, though know I have to be very careful not to cause emotional damage in the way I do. I try as much as possible in front of my daughter to be the "old" dad and very gradually let her see me. Look I am not a child psychologist and had a lot on my plate. I am just doing what seems like a sensible way forward to me. I will adapt. I have to!

My daughter had to face a stranger in the house each time I managed to significantly affect my cognitive function. Of course, we didn't want this but it happened none the less. I want an honest account as she is so, so smart that at some point in the future, when she is ready, she can find out what really happened to her dad and hopefully she will see that some things were happening beneath the visible surface, in a fight to come back home.

On that side, where my daughter knew the vegetable me, it feels so strange to hope, that she will like the real me.  It breaks my heart that I don't know.

# Chapter 10

I was surprised to learn, the skills I had developed when manic to erase part of my life. I don't remember doing this at all but I have several hundred blocked contacts on my phone, most of which I don't know who the people are...

I probably should explain that although I have a great phone my use of it for well talking to people was limited. I realise that some of you are going to question money at this point.

OK I have an iPhone XR. I have a question for iPhone users. How much did you pay for your phone? We don't buy new phones; we buy renewed phones from Amazon (brilliant by the way). I spent 3 weeks looking at every hour of the day, until I caught the pricing at £50 off.

An interesting fact, well again to me it is, is that renewed phones generally are under a reseller type program governed by Amazon but not sold by them. The same guarantees as new phones. Anyway, these sellers seem to release "batches" of phones every 24 hours or so.

Towards the end of the batch if phones are not selling for a few hours, prices are dropped and when first released sometimes for an hour or so, phones are much cheaper. I worked this out myself of course last year. I had time not money you see.

Anyway, I got the phone for maybe 25% of its original retail price at something like 4am in the morning. This was cheaper than a year on a contract for the same phone with one of the telecoms companies. OK we at the moment are not on benefits but everyone needs a phone.

I have loads of other tips for saving money by the way but that's not really why we are here. I just didn't want you thinking that we have loads of money stashed somewhere.

Somehow, I found a way to hide from myself text messages from other people that were not blocked (clever but confused the hell out of me when recontacting people) and I blocked people on various social media sites, as well as other tricks, I didn't know you could do. By that I mean I have no memory of previously knowing.

This is on top of me erasing all information I had stored about phone numbers and email addresses across dozens of backups. I later destroyed all emails from the 6 months around that time space as I couldn't bear to look at them and so cannot refer to any of them.

I have apologised to people already about this blocking/deletion (not that I remember it) but was amazed at the lengths I went to during my mental illness. I can only guess I was trying to protect the people concerned from me.

# Chapter 11

This is hard to write for me. I adjusted to a life without friends (except one, more later), where I would forever be a burden to my family and to just somehow have to deal with that. I have been told many, many times I would not ever be the man I used to be. Not by my wife but by those trying to get me accustomed to my new life.

To be honest people wanted me to get a job stacking shelves in local supermarkets. I am not sure what would have happened if I had and whether it would have affected my recovery but I am guessing it wouldn't have ended well.

Also, as I open this subject my family felt that my failure to progress over the first few years was about things such as fear of the unknown, lack of confidence, anxiety from the medications and the experience.

Fundamentally they felt that in these situations that I could inherently do these things, I just needed the push to do them. This is the logical explanation for many and probably the most likely set of circumstances.

If people listen to nothing else, I write, this idea is nothing to do with my experience. Yes, I was afraid initially (who wouldn't be) but my issues were not that I was in some way restricting myself. It was about my brain not having the physical capability to do something. As soon as I could do something again, I have done it.

That is all I have been relentlessly working on for the last 4 years. I never knew if it would work, I never knew when it started to work, how far it could go. I didn't know it would bring me back to the person I recognise until a few weeks ago.

This just was a fact of my life and I fully expected I would never again be the person I was. For years I was not even sure I would be a functional person in any regard. The turning point was the computer (more later) and a discovery that after about the 1,000th attempt of doing something that I learnt it.

Not everything was as difficult (though I only remember an endless cycle of doing things on computers for years…. I have all the documents archived by month so people can see the changes) and I am thankful I didn't have anything else to do so I didn't give up.

My spreadsheets, in the end I was proud of. Should anyone ever want to see them, let me know. I have put hundreds of times the effort into building them than anything I have ever created in the past and to me if no one else they are a thing of beauty. They are simpler than I used to create but for me it was the equivalent of painting a not bad copy of the Mona Lisa, using only my nose

I got a BBC micro when I was 13 in 1977 (I was working down the cafes every school night and 80-hour weeks on holidays) and paid for it with my brother.

Since that point, I have been intricately involved with computers. You may say I think through them. I often see situations through spreadsheets for example. I have worked with them every day to solve problems since Lotus 123 (before Excel) and I have always used computers every day.

I got my first luggable (pre laptop) in 1990 for 1/10 my significant annual city salary (sorry, don't hate me) as an example because access to computers was so important to me (I could have bought 5-7 good laptops today for the same price, not adjusted for inflation).

I have worked with PCs every day since the IBM AT in 1986 and have been online since 1995, paying more for it than I do now. I do think that this has been my saviour in regards to what happened as it has been the foundation of all my recovery.

I have spent on average over 14 hours a day on the computer (as I have always used computers), constantly carrying out tasks, again and again over the last 3 years.

To explain how this experience felt. My profession, my hobby, my interests, my obsessions all circulated around computers and technology. I had spent over 30 years on them yet suddenly felt I was starting from scratch. To be fair, it didn't feel great.

What I also realised is that it didn't came back the second, or third or 100th time I attempted it. I relearned Excel from almost the start after 30 years of using spreadsheets. That's like asking Kasparov to relearn chess from the beginning and telling him to relearn every move 100 times (not comparing myself to Kasparov! Just an example).

However, I saw after a few months of working on spreadsheets, I gradually regained some of my cognitive abilities albeit at a painful pace so slow I can only believe I had the patience because I didn't have the cognitive mindset to get frustrated.

Over the last 2 years, I have created a wide range of spreadsheets for home, which I constantly change, summarise, revisit for improvements etc. Gradually I felt brain function improve and interestingly as it does, I remember how to do things related to it.

What was also interesting to me was that the creative elements of what I did, grew alongside the functional. I may need to explain but as I created basic spreadsheets to do things, and gradually made these more complex. There was also a correlating gradual improvement in style and looks.

The reason I explain this is that in my mind, I would have guessed that all the logic would come first and the creative elements follow afterwards (i.e., somehow more sophisticated than function) but that didn't happen to me. Both developed, equally slowly.

Those memories seem to me to appear in clumps. Don't know if they do, maybe it's just the realisation hits when there is a lot.

Even after 3 years of working every day on this all day and night, I still don't for example understand any of the VBA (Visual Basic) I used to create. I had programmed for 30 years (initially as a job, then to create management utilities for 20 years and to manage the home) and spent circa 15 years with visual basic so expected that to come back.

I think that may be because I am not sure how to reengage with Visual Basic other than from the beginning. The thought of that is not appealing and I am still more than a little scared I wouldn't be able to do it anyway.

I just realised something, I have mentioned the role of excel and the spreadsheets I maintain which were behind the start of my cognitive redevelopment.

Since returning from hospital, all of these (maybe 15) religiously daily maintained workbooks, which all revolve around energy use dissected in all sorts of ways (Hey you work with what you have got) …. I haven't touched any of them, nada. I have been updating those for many hours a day for years. Isn't that funny. Well to me it is.

# Chapter 12

One of the things I have found very interesting is just how slow it was for me to make the most basic advances in my cognitive skills in the early years and how much that accelerated as those skills sets develop.

I would guess that relates to the brain's connections and neurons, that the more connections that are formed (or reformed) that the quicker subsequent connections are and the easier to find connections that deal with the cognitive function you are looking at.

I will try to find a brain expert that can explain to me what was going on and will provide an update for a later version of the digital book if successful.

Looking back, I realise that my ability to regain function has accelerated dramatically, which I only realised recently. A few months ago, I spent several weeks arguing about Covid with an Anti-Vaxer and a general conspiracy theorist.

That should probably have taken about 20 minutes for me to express my view. However, starved of debate, I didn't let go and luckily for me the person I was dealing with continually responded.

No matter how ridiculous his view, he defended it… not well but he defended it. Each time I broke down the argument and provided a detailed response to every point based on provable science and facts.

We debated for several weeks. I now realise I needed it to develop that side of my brain, so he helped me…. In fact, a lot, I couldn't have written this without him. So regardless of the batshit theories he has I owe him my thanks. I am laughing as I write that as it's so ironic to me.

Anyway, like any well prepped debater, once I refused anymore to watch his Tok-tok videos which he claims is the last refuge of the free… I thought it was make-up videos that were on the app mainly.

I also thought it had a dominant teenage girl audience. I wonder what a grown man was doing on a site for dancing cats looking there for the truth on the world's issues.

He also of course manages to watch conspiracy sites from a wide range of sites. When I say wide range, I think its six. All as he puts it are the last refuge of the truth. Ok I thought, I wonder what those sites are about.

One of them is directly managed by the security services of a large communist country. Will give a hint. I wonder how that is independent.

Now there's this other one. Hmm well I suppose white supremacists have views and maybe some of them are really nice. Like maybe they like puppies and stuff. However little unusual using that as a main source of your views isn't it.

Moving on, this next one looks as though it may be interesting. I wonder what god's army has to do with being unvaccinated. Strange but nice to see its leader though can walk through walls and send millions of his spirit bodies all over the world. That must be nice.

I now recognise myself from before for the first time. Trust me I know I was never perfect but it's nice to be home finally. I am a little like a teenager in how happy I have been about it.

One event changed everything for me recently. I was hospitalised for a gall bladder infection. My hospital ward had no radio, no TV. No-one had newspapers and my phone had no signal so no outside calls (no signal during the day).

No internet, no news, no distractions.

I was placed in a situation where I either sat there for 4 days or engaged. Luckily for me I was in a diagnostic unit (world class) and I was fascinated by how it all worked. So, I started engaging with anyone and everyone about how the place worked.

If I hadn't spent months debating in writing leading up to this, I don't think I would have been able to engage and I was very nervous.

What helped me was that the consultant in charge of me, that directed my case investigation, was one of the smartest people I have ever met. I used to work with some very smart people (more later) and this awoke in me something, to see such raw intelligence in action and applied. It was a wonder to behold and something I haven't seen in a very long time.

As with the rest of the world Covid had happened and opposite me was a patient who had been hospitalised for 61 days and in an induced coma for 3 weeks.

His coma experience was incredible. His mind had created a whole world he lived in for what he perceived as months. He was completely oblivious to the outside world and he said the world was as real as ours is now. Incredible stuff. We spent maybe 10 hours talking about this, I just couldn't ask enough questions.

I will just say (as it fascinates me), that in this world of his he created there were no TV's, radios, newspapers, news of any kind or clocks. All so the mind could contain what it had made. Wow.

Just one more thing on this as everyone will be thinking it, yes of course I watched Life on Mars. He started trying to write about his experiences but felt it was too similar to Life on Mars for him to bother. One day, just maybe if people don't hate my writing style, I will try to contact him about that book.

I also got to speak to someone who worked on the Covid ICU wards in April to July 2020 and that was extremely sad but truly enlightening and fascinating.

During this period, my vocabulary renewed. I probably added 1,000-2,000 words back in my vocabulary in the 4 days I was there. I don't mean I learnt them. I am guessing somehow the neuron links in my brain became reconnected (as they do) and I instantly "re" knew them (including context, usage in my past etc). If only school had been like that.

What I am finding now is that now I have established some of the core building blocks of my cognitive function such as logic and the ability to store and process things, other aspects of my character are easier to redevelop.

From the moment I was on abilify in 2015 I found I could no longer write and I haven't been able to write until very recently because of cognitive reasons. I have been finding that as with spreadsheets that me going through debates on topical subjects has developed my writing skills significantly.

I treated each debate almost as a I would have a work piece and put substantial effort into the dissection of the problem, the analysis and fact checking, the construction of the argument and supporting figures and data. I would spend up to an hour on each piece and spent a large part of my day doing this for nearly two months. I was amazed how much this helped me develop those skills.

However, it was clear that it was only after all the formative work that any of that would have been possible and that had taken years.

What I am also finding and I have no idea if this is common is that memories recently flood over me as I have conversations with people I used to know. Its isn't like I can now access an individual memory but like I am suddenly aware of hundreds at a time. Its like the knowledge comes in waves.

This has been happening over the last few days. I can only imagine that neurons are suddenly more connected and therefore establishing links quicker but I am no expert. What I can say for sure is as I talk to more people the pace of change in my brain has exponentially increased.

Suddenly if I need to do something new that I knew before its seconds, minutes or at worst hours for me to be able to do it not months at a time. I am constantly re-evaluating how far I can now go as the boundaries I expected keep moving to the distance.

This will sound self-obsessed but I actually don't remember how smart I used to be and how far away I am from that. All I know is I am currently one happy bunny and if the changes stopped now, I couldn't complain.

About a week after I had finished the book, these changes just one day stopped. As far as I can tell I can cognitively do everything I could before but in some ways my brain processes things i.e., problem solving is slightly different to how it was before.

The changes never occurred since. It was almost as though my brain knew the job was done. I am sure someone will tell me this is impossible. I lived through this however and the difference was night and day.

# Chapter 13

.

I had lucid moments in the haze of madness I went through in 2015 and in the short period (lasted a week or so) in which I wrote, which was whilst also suffering a constant state of mania, one thing I can stand looking at may give insight to my mind at the time.

I was writing amongst other things (God knows why) odes to people, most of whom I admired and I wrote one about Stephen Fry. Everyone knows what a wonderful spokesman he is for mental health. He is in short, a legend.

I will reproduce that ode. I do not claim anything of it. I don't hate it. I am not a poet and had never written anything like it before my mania or since. Maybe you will see something from it I can't about my state of mind.

## Stephen Fry

More than just IQ
Took several incredibly difficult subjects and embraced them
Personal maybe, misunderstood definitely
Someone, somewhere has to stand up and shout about the complexities of life
With the flair of Dave Allen, A little brush of the clothes, A little smile
The issues that cause so much pain are aired
He wasn't afraid to be different yet the subjects could be terrifying
He wasn't afraid to be unique
He stood tall, when others bow their heads
Hope is given to so many

You have helped me embrace that which is different about me
Why be the same, when we can be unique?

My little bit about the above. First, it's one of my few good memories of the time. As part of my manic period, I looked up his management agency and submitted this to them. They came back to me saying he had read it and liked it. I don't have those emails, I destroyed everything from that period but remember that clearly.

Actually, I will put a section in the back of the book of some of my writings during this period leading up to and immediately after my initial breakdown. It will probably give insight to someone. I will write what I see but I covet any opinion (no matter how out there) people have about this stuff as to how it relates to state of mind.

A bit more about my writing. I reached a point where I was going to insert the writing I did during my breakdown and extended mania. I have realised 24 hours later that I keep avoiding doing it. I didn't realise at first, I just found other things to do and then convinced myself that the next step instead was getting feedback and talking to people.

Truth was I could have done all that and progressed. I found myself wanting to watch the news or a TV program. I realised subconsciously it's me trying to avoid doing this. I'm still self-indulging and weighing up the benefits of waiting until I feel comfortable or forcing myself.

Neither sound appealing. However, I know I will never be ready to look at that stuff. I know what I have to do. Wish me luck. I will let you know if it was as bad as I thought. By the way you will see a lot of me mocking the writing. I know it's a coping mechanism but I will try to tell the truth.

I had never before writing this book, sat back and thought through everything that had happened. I hadn't attempted to understand it at all. I think I never would have if I hadn't fully recovered.

I started this book within a week or two of knowing that I was me again however so deep down, maybe I knew I needed to do this.

Back in 2015 I had never written anything outside work before and suddenly I decided I was a writer. Strangely that is the one thing that has stuck with me, I truly enjoy writing now. I honestly don't know whether I would have thought about it otherwise. I hadn't prior to 2015.

I actually entered into negotiations with one specialist book publisher in 2015, with discussion about an advance. That was until I demanded a year's salary worth of advance. At that point they asked more questions, deduced I wasn't quite right and stopped answering my calls. How embarrassing.

I struggled so much just even looking at what I wrote in 2015. Whilst many people were very pleasant about what I wrote all I see in what I wrote at the time is the madness running through me. However maybe I am biased.

I learnt a few techniques with business writing I used from some clever people, early on in my career and it seemed to stand me in good stead.

I would summarise that in a few phrases. Keep it simple (as you can) and Easy reading makes hard writing. i.e., that the effort in writing alleviates the effort in reading. A quote I love in regards to both written and spoken conversation is "Communication is about both people understanding what has been said".

There is also a key one. Speak from the Heart.

# Chapter 14

Another set of strange facts. For the last 6.5 years I have watched the television. It was the way I passed the time from waking until sleeping. Fundamentally, it the TV was on from when I get up to when I get to bed. For me, one of my greatest concerns was what happens if the TV breaks down, especially in the earlier years. That makes me laugh actually.

Anyway, since I came back home from hospital, I haven't watched the TV at all. It's on with the news in the background but apart from catching up on After Life (brilliant by the way) I haven't seen anything. That 4 days in hospital when I had to use my brain, seems to have reset me in some way. Well, my brain had one hell of a rest. About time.

Another revealing moment for me was that my daughter entered a speaking competition last year. She did well and came in the medals. I watched it a number of times last year and enjoyed it and thought she did well. I sent that video recently to my friends I had reconnected with and thought well why not watch it again myself.

It was a revelation. I was blown away how smart, well expressed and how thoughtfully connected it was. It flowed from subject to subject seamlessly. I mean (slightly biased maybe) it was brilliant. It was a completely different experience.

I watched it 4 times with pride. I thought that part of my brain was working last year but it was like going from a spiderman home movie to a £250 million pound experience. The interesting thing is I really didn't know how much my cognitive function had developed in that space without that comparison. I was surprised by how much I had changed.

One of the nice things about what's happening is that historical memories are also getting better again i.e. I can access more. I missed those memories a lot.

One other funny thing, I don't recall anyone new I have spoken to, asking me about the hospital stay stuff (for my Gall Bladder). I mean it's all medically fine and I am recovering well but that makes me happy. They have been more interested in me as I have been gone so long to them. I assume as well it means that they are happy with the engagement from me. My gall bladder can wait!

One of my best friends said it was like you pressed pause in 2015 and play in the last 2 weeks. I like that a lot. That is actually, in many regards what it feels like.

# Chapter 15

I had previously spent 15 years as a management consultant and at the time this all happened, I was in a job I loved with a passion.

Whilst at work, for the first time in my life, I felt an overwhelming dizziness worse than if I had been turned around 100 times on the spot and left to walk afterwards. I was sitting down so knew this was not right. This was about 10am.

I had a key meeting (sort of once in a year, cannot miss) in the afternoon or I would have gone back to the room I was staying at. I started experiencing blurriness in my eyes and couldn't read and my thinking was affected. This went on for several hours until the meeting.

The HR director in the meeting stopped it as they couldn't communicate with me (they said it was like I had phased out completely) and the HR Director drove me back to where I was staying during the week (though I don't remember that). I should say, I loved this job at the time and was having key meetings constantly. I was desperate to be there.

That night I started getting extreme stomach pains every hour or two and had to go to the toilet urgently. By the next morning I knew it was so severe and so frequent I couldn't work and agreed with them that I would return home.

When home the pains got worse, the visits to the toilet continued and then the blood started after a few days. First just a bit and then a lot. Blood started literally pouring from me (up to ½ pint each time) for a number of days (close to a week I think) every time I went to the toilet (which was every hour or so day and night for over a week).

I went to the hospital and then via 111 the emergency doctors at the hospital in the middle of the night because I was so concerned about this (which you can understand with blood pouring from me). In both instances it was agreed it was just a burst set of blood vessels.

Over a two-week period, I couldn't sleep because of these hourly sudden pains in my stomach (even after the blood stopped) and at the end of this period I still was getting the pains without going to the toilet.

At the time I thought it must be muscle memory or something that woke me up with a jolt even if I had managed to sleep and forced me to go to the toilet instantly (literally with 30 seconds notice). I estimated at that time I slept an average of 2 hours a night for nearly 2 weeks.

I have a very vague memory of my sister coming round to see a film. I have no idea what the film was but my memory was that in the few hours we were together I had to go to the toilet several times.

Some people can survive on 2 hours sleep for 2 weeks. I couldn't and I was deteriorating. My wife and daughter were in Japan with a dying mother and a father that didn't even know. I hid what was happening as to put additional burdens wasn't fair.

I should explain about what was happening to my brain at this point. Whilst I was deathly tired my brain was suddenly crystal clear from near the start of the illness at home. I had only had such clarity when

I was much younger and my brain was at its peak (late teens/early twenties).

I found I could solve problems quicker and actually did some really advanced work initially from home (it was confirmed as such by work). At this point even now, I remember that clarity. It only became a warped clarity many days in.

I didn't understand why my mind could race and be so clear and yet I was so, so tired I could barely stay awake but put this down to some sort of adrenaline rush from the physical illness.

Some of what I put in the following I struggle to put exact timelines to. It all happened but the sequencing may have been slightly different.

I became more and more involved in social media (I think maybe as I was alone and awake and struggling for some interaction or feedback I guess).

I don't remember exactly what I did cover but I know I got involved in supporting Obamas official page which was supporting Hilary Clintons campaign and too closely followed a captain of industries website and commented on every major announcement.

At the time I was pleased as Obama's team continually bumped my posts up on Facebook so it remained visible amongst thousands of posts. I am guessing at that time I must still have made some form of sense though I shudder to think) and I don't remember posting them.

Things came off the rails after that and there was a 24-hour period where I felt tired beyond belief, but where I was truly manic where I must have written 1,000 emails alone (everyone at work and my friends started blocking me, at work first individually on my personal email addresses then they blocked me corporately on their servers after initially indulging me.

I have just remembered I switched emails to avoid these blocks. Man was I stupid.

I accused a captain of industry of kidnap (of who I can't remember) and started posting across dozens of his sites. His team were quick to catch and remove (thankfully) and never pursued me over it. I learnt a new respect for him that day.

An update on the above. After 6.5 years I sent an apology to the address most given on the web (and it looks right). However, it bounced. I sent to another senior person asking them to forward and no response. I suppose it looks a bit weird an apology after 6.5 years.

Apparently, I also pretended to be my brother when other people called my phone. I wrote some fairly rude, sweary emails to former colleagues via LinkedIn and unknowingly copied all several hundred of my senior contacts.

Unsurprisingly I was banned from LinkedIn!  I just want to say that was the first thing I have ever in my life been banned from.   It still stings!

After that I slept like a log.  When I awoke the pain had stopped in my stomach and I knew immediately that whether it was a breakdown or psychotic episode I knew I had had an event.

I contacted 3 mental health charities to discuss that next day, with the rest of the day dedicated to deleting messages I had sent.  Years later I discovered some of these messages. I couldn't read them I had to just delete them.

To give an idea of the voracity of the illness I lost over 15kg.

# Chapter 16

My relationship with sleep continued to be strained after the breakdown and its impact on me continued unabated.

The following day, I ate healthily and went for drinks with a Friend. However, I lost feeling in my cheek and left hand and drove to A&E. Looking back, I must have done something as they alerted the Mental Health Team to see me.

I have a vague memory of freezing at moments involuntarily almost robotically as I walked to be seen but not sure whether that is a false memory. There is no doubt however I had been through a breakdown and it's not unreasonable to imagine that this showed.

I was given a standard questionnaire and laughed my way through it. Does the TV talk to you, do you hear voices outside your door? You can imagine the flippant answers. At the time I thought the issue had passed but something obviously and clearly was wrong and visibly so.

The next day I was visited at home, which at the time I found strange but for some reason just thought they were hassling me. This is part of the standard engagement process for the mental health team. I was alone, I had had a breakdown and I could not have showed coping processes.

Just on this I just remembered I started hassling all of the oversight boards of the Mental Health teams, including its Chief executive. I also then contacted (wow this has just come back) the CEO office of the organisation that previously had responsibility for mental health provision about exerting pressure for them to cease and desist.

It was the CEO of a massive UK company with tens if not hundreds of thousands of employees. I don't remember who that was but I am pretty sure I remember he responded (saying it was not his problem any more or something).

I have deleted all this stuff so I may have inaccuracies. I have a history of pressing CEO offices when I fail to get a response from organisations, so guess it was on autopilot or more scarily I still had my logic without its sense of direction.

This will explain yet more reasons why they thought I wasn't right. Wow did I give them fuel. Well, if I am going to go a bit bonkers for a bit, may as well go full in.

The mental health team is notoriously late for almost all meetings (not their fault but I didn't know anything about them then). When late for me I refused their meetings. I did not realise that refusing to engage when they are worried about you is a bad move. I did this a few times.

The next call was from the Police who this time arrived with the team on my doorstep unannounced. I was in the pub. I said I would be home at 11pm. I thought I was being clever and was quite pleased with myself at the time. Oh well. You can't teach stupid.

Apparently, my friend arrived from the other side of London and I was shoeless, sockless in the pub and he said looked like I had had a shower in my clothes. I guess I was also running a fever.

When he met me, the barmaid gave him a free pint and said he would need it. What followed was I berated and derided my friend, who was someone I had shared a job with across three organisations for over 10 years. Shameful. Thankfully he has forgiven me.

Apparently at one stage, we were having a competition (I had forced it) and I said name a subject and I will ask a question on it. When it was my turn apparently, I chose Quantum Mechanics and reeled off a technical question in elaborate detail where my friend was convinced, I knew the subject. The only fact I know about Quantum Mechanics is how to spell it.

Actually, I have to update. My friend at this moment is on a corporate all-day videoconference and I have been sending him cartoons about Quantum Mechanics to make him laugh. I came across ones (I guess I can't reproduce those) about the duality of Schrödinger's cat. I actually know that theory.

Amazing what you forget. I wonder when I found out about Quantum Mechanics and why I did. I mean it's not like a subject you think oh right I better read up on that.

I didn't realise I knew something about Quantum mechanics…. So maybe after all I did ask a real question (90% though I would guess as being made up). To be fair I could have been talking about mass spectrometry and he would have said it sounded accurate. If its geeky, he switches off. Football or After Life or Ronnie Corbett impressions and he is all in though.

Just on this as to me it's funny. Myself and my friend are now back in contact and I tease him about the Quantum Mechanic thing (easier than continually blushing). I have decided to read up on it so that I can wind him up a little as a reminder. My humour is not for everyone….

I had said to the Police I would be at home at 11. They met me there. Maybe 12am. There was obviously a concern but I didn't know what it was at the time and didn't care. From what my friend experienced and what I just remembered above the outcome was predictable.

# Chapter 17

The following day, I was awoken at 9am by a mental health assessment team who had the power to section me. I didn't know why they did this but now retrospectively would plead no contest. A friend (was then, understandably not now) drove down from Birmingham (a 3-hour drive) to be there.

I shudder to remember how I treated him. It was shameful. He rightly was telling me I need help and I should go with them. All I could see was him abandoning me. I berated and admonished him constantly. All he was trying to do was help. I still cringe when I think of it, which is not often as I can't stand to do so.

I have actually written to him to try to apologise, three times. Which probably looks a little like I am stalking him. I am not by the way.

I now know the erratic behaviours I had been exhibiting and I will clearly say on reflection that a mental health facility was where I needed to be and quick. I chose to go voluntarily to avoid the locked doors of sectioning.

Whilst a mental health ward is never a place anyone wants to be and was in itself a truly scary experience, it was the only place I needed to be at that time. The staff I was in daily contact with were incredible.

The zombification of the drugs given in the first few days was probably necessary and the treatment at that time appeared to work, although throughout my first stay this feeling of absolute clarity at key times remained, even when I was discharged.

I started writing a book, which though others like to read, I hate to see as it triggers memories of my state of mind. It did however help me as it sequenced events by day.

I should say though this is where things get strange. Everything seemed to slow down in the Mental Health Assessment unit for me. Being with a group of highly susceptible people for an extended period creates group situations where theories intertwine and develop, where these are not real, they can be quite scary.

These theories are all whispered and spoken amongst the patients, out of sight of the staff. It is the only time I ever experienced any sort of group collective impact. I don't generally care what anyone else thinks. No that's not fair, I care deeply. I mean I don't need anyone else in the world to agree with me normally.   My opinion is deeply my own.

At that time (and I will merge hospital stays and the intervening period as exact recollection of timing for me is impossible) I believed for a period: -

- There was a group of angels on the ward (the other people also believed the same thing by the way)
- That the way they sat or arched their backs indicated if they were a good angel or bad angel (I think maybe I was channelling Constantine with Keanu Reeves)
- That god could talk to me through wasps in the mental health garden and that I could do the reverse
- That the tree in our mental health garden was from the garden of Eden and represented good and evil.
- That our guinea pigs at home were angels sent from Heaven to protect me (I know one was Gabriel and the other Michael but for the life of me don't know now which one it was.  Sorry guys)

- That messages were being sent by God through the songs played on Smooth Radio (why did God send that particular song)

I will say this and though I cannot prove it, I truly believe it, this time of my mind racing and intense warped clarity (I thought I could close my eyes and feel the universe – really) and I believed I had an intelligence I had never before possessed and that I was intricately connected to the universe. I have never felt so much although I knew it wasn't right.

In some strange ways I think I did have some form of additional controls. I found I could suddenly control my heart rate and instantly think through things I had never been able to before. It wasn't just an illusion. Whilst it may not have been real, elements of it were.

All of this mind racing (which by this stage was a period of several weeks) came at a very heavy cost. I believe this time somehow was causing massive brain damage to me as when it stopped, everything had gone and it never came back (until a few weeks ago, several years later).

I honestly had such access to my brain that I never had, it was like could access all of it at once and then the light switch went off.

Again, this will sound strange but during this period of warped clarity I could feel there was something wrong with my brain. I don't know how else to describe this in any way that will make sense.

However, it was probably the strangest sensation I ever had and even now freaks me out a little to think of.

I was lost though in what was happening to me. I would never have imagined it was possible but my thinking whilst bizarre didn't allow for logic to enter the equation, it's like that whole part of my brain had shut off. I could still interact but the guidance system wasn't being controlled by me. I don't know what part but I was an observer after a while to the experience.

The crash to earth, from which it has taken several years to recover a significant part of me was like the before and after of a nuclear bomb. Afterwards there was nothing.

And there was also a host of some dark stuff on the wards that populates nightmares from the very first days there, some of it very, very real. Additionally, some truly very sick i.e., ill people (some of who claimed to be Satan or his minions) gained traction with me and others to scare us about what was happening and left me unable to sleep for days.

It is only in this suggestible state that you listen to these things but to me, having never been scared by these things, I was more scared than I had ever been since I was a teenager watching the Exorcist alone, where everyone else went to bed and left me watching it at a party.

Since that period of 2015, I haven't watched any truly scary stuff on film. A lot of horror isn't really. Although I still haven't watched really scary stuff, I stopped being afraid of it as my cognitive skills redeveloped (I would guess maybe 18 months ago). I think I am probably now in a place I could watch the exorcist again.

What will scare me is not the film but it will evoke memories of being on the mental health ward and the people who claimed to be the devil, especially the guy who whispered in my ear.

There was quite a few claiming this or that they were the messiah (it's surprising how many believe this) and even in a normal state they would have scared me, as when they ranted it was worse and more disturbed than anything I have seen on film, especially when they focused on me (one guy used to whisper in my ear stuff that still makes me shiver in fear). However, in the fragile state I was in I was terrified for much of my stay, though I never discussed that with anyone.

It led me to check with people that visited me whether they were with the Devil. A strange thing for someone who doesn't believe in the devil (well I truly thought I don't).

I also had the rather peculiar experience for a day where every face I saw on TV had Howard from the Big Bang Theory superimposed on it. There was a lot of other stuff like this but to be honest it blurs into the background for me, though I know it went on.

Enough said. I needed to be there. The places terrified me as some of the people's behaviour can be scary stuff, especially when you are not well. However, all the staff were brilliant everywhere in all their roles in supporting you and helping you recover, except for one nurse who used to try to scare me every time I asked to charge my phone by talking about the scary patients who were really something evil (knowing about my fears).

# Chapter 18

It was raised by a doctor on the ward at the time how unusual it was for a 51-year-old to present with my symptoms for the first time and that they thought it should be investigated for other physical causes. No-one ever did.

No-one attempted to understand why I would present at such a late stage in my life when most of these mental health conditions (especially for example Bi-Polar) exhibit from late teens onwards.

No-one delved at any point as to whether I had for example other episodes in my life even untreated, no one looked into other causes.

I was released way before I was ready to go home, purely because my Wife and Daughter had returned from Japan, I ended up back in hospital within a few days. This was treated as a separate event and as such I was medicated differently. Instead of being on medication until the issues resolved I was put on them with a view to multi-year use.

I never had these issues before, I have never had them since, I left the hospital and within a few days was back in because I was not at all ready to have left. However, this is categorised, I speak from being the person involved it was the same episode. Hence when it was over after the second hospitalisation I never went back, in the same way I was never there before.

The danger is that to the lazy, this is the medication working. The medication is preventing the episodes i.e., that is why I didn't have episodes during that period.

# Chapter 19

I was put on monthly injectable abilify which was reduced to minimum dosage after a few years. Every month I complained of intense brain fog (I think I used to say I couldn't think and sometimes I couldn't process).

Every month it was reported. It was strange I remember going to get my monthly abilify injection and sitting in the office more clearly than almost anything else in that 2016/2017 period.

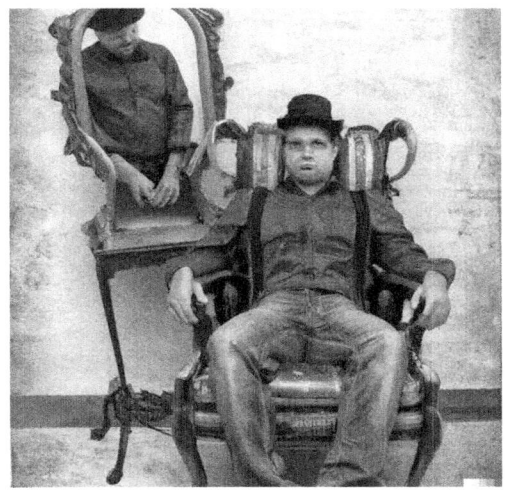

It was made clear to me by the doctors I was not going to be taken off the medication, with a clear determination that this was forever.

My sister helped me a lot. I decided to come off the drugs. I did however lie about my trail off of abilify to everyone though with my own reasons.

I started to suspect that stopping abilify alone would not magically bring me back and was scared of what would happen if my family realised that I may never be the same. I realised this because as abilify itself was reduced my immediate brain function didn't improve an iota.

I should explain. At this time, we knew I wasn't me (fairly obvious differences me compared to vegetable). However, we thought the evil abilify was completely to blame, in all regards.

My family hoped that as I tapered off the drug, I would return to myself. At that stage to be honest, I didn't have an opinion as I wasn't capable of one.

I told my family I was reducing the drug sensibly at 3-month intervals by 25%. I didn't I reduced to ½ one month then stopped completely. This gave me 7 months to try to figure out if I was coming back whilst my family thought I was trailing off. I am amazed I thought that through at the time as my processing capability at the time was limited.

I knew 7 months before them I wasn't coming back. Those 7 months I was very anxious as I wasn't sure what would happen to us as a family once, they knew.

I erratically collected the tablets to match what I had told my family before to appear as though I was still taking them. So, my doctors believe I remained on abilify for maybe nearly 12 months longer than I did.

I don't remember the last injection but that was the last time I took those tablets properly and for the declaration that was my intention. The reason I mention that is that once during my mental health experience I ran out of abilify.

The way the Mental Health unit worked often you didn't get the new set of tablets until the day your last set ran out (on the day itself). I ran out and was waiting on a new set and had gone past the time to take them. I found remnants of 2 pills from being on the unit and took these rather than nothing, while I waited on a new set of tablets (they were only 7 days at a time). That was a mistake

I was registered as unreliable and put on mandated injectable abilify as I was not trusted anymore to take tablets.

I never want to see abilify again in my life. I make no claim as to its impact on others but to me, it is the drug from hell that took 3 years of my life.

The drug may not have been the cause of my brain not working (it was brain damage).  Abilify stopped my brain from forming new neuron pathways and rebuilding connections in some way.  That is why I stayed a complete vegetable until after I stopped abilify and why I cannot remember virtually anything for the years I was on it.

I will also make clear I never want to be treated as though I have a constant ongoing lifelong mental illness again unless it is demonstrated and proven it is the case and that physical causes are not at play.

It was purely convenient for the doctors and as I wasn't really there, I couldn't properly defend myself and for that no one cared.

# Chapter 20

My real issue starts after I left hospital. Once the mental issues subsided, I was left with an all-encompassing brain fog. You can ask my sister, my wife or anyone that dealt with me but basically, I was initially (for years 2016-Mid 2018) incapable of stringing a coherent thought or sentence. I couldn't properly express myself other than to say I couldn't think and that looking back on it is exactly what it was. I couldn't think.

I cannot express how this stripped and stole from me the time, every joy, every thought, every experience, including beautiful memories of my daughter growing up in what should have been a supportive family. I stopped being able to be a father. That hurt me more than I can say.

Even now my daughter struggles to recognise the changes in me as they are so disorientating. She in her formative years knew me as a vegetable. It wasn't what she wanted but what she had so my wife and daughter dealt with that.

Over the last 2 years and especially the last 18 months, I keep changing as I keep getting mental faculties back. I would compare it to buying a normal rat which lives with you for several months, then suddenly it starts singing showtunes from Hamilton. Very impressive but it is going to make you feel very uncomfortable.

For my daughter who doesn't know this me it's like a stranger in the house. The fact that others I am now talking to me only know this version of me, is even more disorientating. The fact I suddenly have friends in my life again she doesn't really remember is yet another jar.

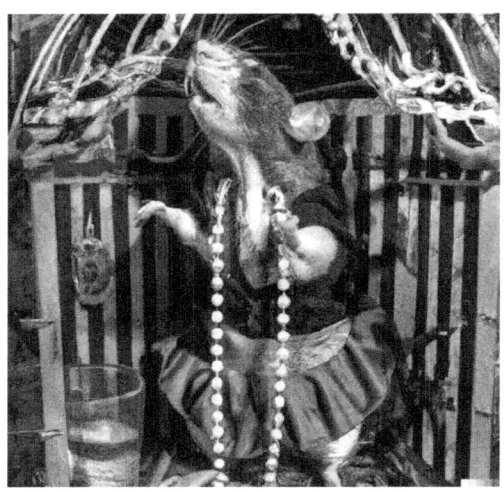

I can't explain how this vegetative state I was in tore at my relationships with people, or how it made me afraid to deal with others or the outside world when I had always been outgoing.

It was also devastating on my wife, my sister, my daughter who had to live with a virtual vegetable. I lost every friend I had in my life but one (who was really my dad's friend and never knew me at work) by my choice.

I should explain anyone that knew me at work, that was a friend of me there, knew me as bright, a rapid thinker, I engage rapidly and analyse and deduce quickly. I couldn't expose myself to people that knew me like that.

My dad's friend just knew me from a pint and had no expectations from me at all.  My wife and sister were so worried about me in 2016/2017 onwards they encouraged me to meet once a week and so we did.  How he coped with a vegetable sipping a pint, for several months on end, that was uncommunicative I don't actually know.

He is the type (like my dad was) that doesn't talk about these things so I guess I will never know.  When I was divorced and I was in pieces, my dad only said "we don't have to talk about this do we?".  That's the nature of my dad's friend who has become my friend.

I will say he was with me throughout this process from the first mental health interview, week in, week out until now but although I have asked, he doesn't want to say anything, feels uncomfortable being asked and I respect that.  He never did what he did in the anticipation of reward, which is a sign of a good friend.

I was dysfunctional and from being the brightest person in any room (this is what I have been told throughout my life), I engaged as much as furniture does. I could not stand for people to see me as a nothing person, who has no ideas, beliefs or even words.

It's a little like locked in syndrome, where you can see everything but cannot express anything. However, in my case I could see but not process, by that I mean I saw stuff going on in front of me but didn't even process it.

It was beyond not understanding it, it never went in in the first place. It didn't get processed later or slowly. I was just a video camera without a memory card, with as much intelligence or understanding as that camera would have.

From 2016/2017 I remember being taken to the park by my sister and the seafront and a local museum. I remember trying to express how I couldn't form thoughts as we walked on the pier. I still don't know if I did that (I must ask). All those memories just didn't quite form and in that period most of them didn't at all.

People have asked me if I was scared in the early years and I had never really thought about that. I didn't have fear as such, without understanding what is there to fear. I had extreme anxiousness if I had to do anything as I knew I couldn't.

I have struggled to explain the next bit but will do what I can for now. Somehow, I knew I wasn't me, though it wasn't me thinking these things. I can only imagine that somehow the mind and the body are sending signals to each other but at this moment have no idea.

When going through the awful Employment and Support Allowance process (shameful how the government treat its disabled) my wife and sister had to write applications for me. Much later I discovered and read these.

I never mentioned to either I had seen them (I think they assumed they were thrown away) but they made me break down in tears as it was laid plain what a burden I had been at that time.

At one point apparently the fundamentals of where the toilet was had been lost on me. Luckily not every time but one time is too many. No matter the circumstances it felt to me like it would if I had done this on purpose but hopefully helps indicate the size of the issue I faced. As you might expect I have no recollections of this but that was par for the course.

For me what was weird during that period, is I discovered in my sleep, I could think. I couldn't logically process an argument (who does in dreams I wonder… maybe Ally McBeal) but I could make choices and I could engage in my dreams.

I cosseted that. I didn't want to get up to nothingness. I assume this is a different part of the brain and the fact I remembered that. I don't know if dream memories are the same as normal memories in how they are stored but for me that was my escape from my world.

My brother began to phone me regularly from New Zealand. I don't know when that started but he called every 4-12 weeks. I remember not being able to answer properly but not what was said.

I know mainly he talked to me, the way you would someone in a coma when they can't answer you. It was very reassuring. I think I may also have had a stammer at this point.... I don't know why I place those two things together. I will ask my brother for a later version.

I couldn't retain knowledge, so given the most basic instructions for an extremely long time I couldn't do them. I ate from cold tins for more than 2.5 years if my wife was not there to cook for me as I could not anymore use the stove or the oven. I just couldn't initially process how to work them, how to do things or remember what I had been told.

It's probably very difficult to believe that, somehow you can't learn to turn a knob. I don't completely understand it myself and whilst the above all stands; I do not know if anything else was also

happening. As I struggle to access this period from what I can access I think I just wasn't processing how to do things, anything I mean.

We had gone from a relatively traditional family to one where my wife was my carer. Not only did she lose my ability to physically do things, instantly she lost her companion in any regards and any ability to communicate. This during a period where she lost both her parents and at same time had to ensure our daughter was looked after and protected.

Although there was nothing I could do, I want to hang my head in shame. I wasn't capable of being there when she needed me most. I somehow absorbed this and the feelings to go with it. The intense feelings remain even now as I can never make that situation up and it just isn't fair to my wife.

My wife and daughter. I have danced round talking about what my wife thinks and to be honest, she has yet to read this document. I will say what I perceive as whenever we discuss this, the conversation changes. I hope to add her perspective though if she chooses not to read, I think I know why.

My wife was dumped with a horrific future and had to make the best of it not knowing which way it would turn. My wife got on with this despite losing both her mother and father and whilst one of her beloved brothers went through some truly awful times.

She had a useless vegetable but took on the mantel of running both the household and all aspects of its running. Not knowing ever whether this vegetable would change my wife navigated the three of us through unknowns on a constant basis.

Tiny aspects that this were happening seeped through to me, but it was like asking a hand dryer in Tesco washroom to assist, there was nothing there.

My memory during my mental issues after I had lost warped clarity…. We were sitting by the door and I was melting down before going back in to the mental health wards (within days). The front door was open (I don't know why) and I was shouting I couldn't cope.

My wife for the only time since it happened expressed how she had just lost her parents and was struggling (I think at this stage my wife's beloved Mother had died and her father was dying). This is the only time in 21 years my wife has ever said such a thing.

Anyway, I just couldn't do anything. My wife never mentioned it to me ever again and I have never lost that shame of not being there for her. I hope my wife forgives me using this. Otherwise, I will remove from a later version when she has read it.

At this stage that breakdown (I think it was the only one) was in front of my extremely clever daughter who at the time was 9. From that point my wife ensured that my daughter would not see that element of her father that may frighten her.

For me, I just tried to exist. For my wife and daughter, it was like dealing with advanced dementia. It is so difficult to explain what this felt like, I lost my sense of self, I was aware I was non-functional but couldn't really do anything to express.

The one thing I found I could say and clung to was that I couldn't think. It was as though my brain in the most part had ceased to exist.

This wasn't a transient issue. It lasted years and I raised it every time I saw anyone from the mental health community. It was so severe I qualified for benefits given to those that cannot function (set a timer, boil a kettle, use the stove for either mental or physical reasons) for many months. My sister can describe how limited you need to be qualified for these benefits.

There are two levels, one in which you seek work. I was judged by the DSS as being incapable of such work. When I was interviewed by the DSS I had to have a mental health worker with me to argue for me and to write it down, so later I knew what happened. Very bizarre.

A lot of people initially and understandably became very irritated with me. It was as though I should be able to fix it and start being myself again. From my part, I wasn't there and did not have the cognitive function to have any idea of what to do.

It's as though I fell back just on the basic idea of existence and in the little, I could process just tried to live each day. I have never believed in suicide but if I had at this point, I was an unfair burden on those I loved.

An example of how I functioned is that despite having no interest in cycling (I mean I hate it) for 2 years (2016 and 2017) I watched major cycling events like Tour de France and La Vuelta. I would watch these for up to 8 hours a day or more for several weeks.

Looking back, I liked the fact that I supported one team (Team Sky) with one set of colours and found the constant moving but nothing happening reassuring. Even after watching this though I wouldn't at the time have been able to recall who won.

I also (and I haven't told people this), lost my ability to form detailed memories. I would watch a TV series (even up to 2 years ago), then be able to watch it completely again as I couldn't remember anything that happened.

When I could start using the computer again and speak sentences, I would have to look up what happened If anyone asked.

If myself and my wife watched a TV show, I would watch it multiple times the following day to try to cement it in my memory. The strange thing is I can't remember if that worked, though I did it many, many times. Strange how the mind works.

My memory has recovered somewhat, though I can't recall recent things in the way I can recall older events. I do have memory but it's never been as good since the event. I often now need triggers to recollect things.

Strangely since I started writing this, my memory has improved in making connections. Maybe the sheer process of writing this is forcing neuron connection.

Since it was my brain affected and since it ravaged my ability to think, despite always being in work and in demand before, I haven't worked since. Work was a massive part of my life

On the medication no-one did anything except once a year say review my dosage, which was gradually over 3 years reduced. I continually stated that I couldn't function properly and no one listened or investigated.

I asked to come off the medication as it was the only difference (other than the episode) to before and I was vegetative (I didn't use those words, just I can't think) and I was continually turned down.

As I said it wasn't as though this was me being slightly affected for years, I was basically an empty shell. It affected me so badly I didn't even log onto a computer for nearly 2 years, after nearly 35 years using them for several to up to 14 hours a day every day. I was scared of doing that as I couldn't process their workings anymore.

When I say their workings, what I mean is I stopped understanding how computers worked. I studied computer science for A level and had been in charge of big migration programs so had an integral knowledge of how they function, which helped me a lot in their use.

However, when this happened, that disappeared. I would find myself trying to understand the ramifications of say switching the computer on and remain flummoxed.

As I have said before computers were at the centre of my being since childhood. I am going to explore this fear of them a little as it must be significant (to me anyway). I wouldn't turn the computer on. I remember being afraid of that.

Normally my desire to do things would have ridden roughshod over that but it didn't. My desire to use the computer wasn't there, I think I knew I wouldn't be able to do anything once I got there. Now that makes sense if the reward isn't there why risk the fear.

I had apparently a raft of fears in late 2015 (note I don't go to late 2015 as I don't remember it). Apparently, I developed a fear of knives and I know I had a fear of sleeping tablets (I thought that they made me disappear when I took them and that scared me).

I am not sure why I was worried there wasn't much to disappear. I also don't know why I remember that fact clear as day when I don't remember anything else of that time.

You may wonder, why I broke the fourth wall and chatted to you. I mean you are not here with me now. In some places like Fleabag, it works great. Most of the time it's a bad move.

The reason was to share this experience and to give me someone I could talk to about these things many faced for the first time since they happened.

# Chapter 21

The last part of this journey has mainly been fun with some challenges. I am actually really pretty happy about everything. I don't hate anyone or resent what's happened. Again, not anything altruistic, it just doesn't matter to me anymore. I can't change it.

I don't know if I do this justice but what I want is in some small way for you to feel what I am feeling. We may not be in the same timeline but I just hope that is the experience you get. I deliberately wrote this book as I evaluated everything that happened to me for the first time and I hope that sense of discovery comes across.

One of my objectives with this book was to encapsulate everything about this period, so I can feel its covered and move on. For it to almost take on board my personality and be like talking to me at the time I had recovered. Almost like a sentient being. Of course, I know it's not but still.

Whilst my experience is unusual, I do hope someday, somewhere it may provide solace to someone. If it does, I will be chuffed. I hope you sense the personality of the book itself. If you think that's nonsense, well what do I know.

As I approach the end of the book, I am struggling a little. Not the writing, that flows as usual. Just maybe a bit reticent to finish.

Now this could be two things. I don't want to stop writing the book or the other, I feel I have done my part and this book now doesn't need me. I better explain.

Obviously when I complete this, our exchange has finished. Believe it or not by the way, as I write this, I visualise you here. Brain stuff, I guess. However, I realise that the minute I type the last word it's over.

However. I will stroke this book when its published (like that cat in Austin Powers... or was it a hairy wig) as to me and me only, it's the closest thing to being me at this moment in time, next to my daughter.

I kind of need to close the chapter on this part of my life. I hope I haven't been dark at all. However, this part of my life wasn't all a party. There is some sadness and hurt here.

I'm a positive guy generally and I don't want to dwell on the past. Don't worry these pages will always be here as will I preserved during this amazing period of my life. I will forever treasure my time here. You would not believe how much it has helped me and how cathartic the whole experience is.

I think it has helped me just to deal with and write about things exactly as I experienced them, warts and all. Putting it all on the table just helped.

I kind of hope in some way you see me as a kind of friend (for your time here, of course) and you can feel part of this experience I had with me and I hope you can see the positivity that I have towards the future.

This experience really has taught me to focus on the future and to be thankful that I have it. Just the ability to write this book for instance, which I would never have done if it wasn't for what happened. I would have been immersed in my work until retirement.

What happened made me rethink my life. I may be financially worse off but I have a peace I never had before. My life was a constant hectic stream of change from which I never got to sit and really reflect on whether I was happy.

I was never traditional; I have always found my own way and whilst I admire great structural books. My own feelings about conforming to that structure. I can sum It up in one word. meh

Let's keep this our book, done our way. After all it was my life. Can't I choose how to talk about it (the answer to that is probably no). However, I live in hope.

Don't worry whatever happens I will be here, waiting for you to come visit me. I am not going anywhere. Visit anytime, night or day.

Isn't that how I should end this book? Yes, yes, it is.

# Afterword

Nearly a year later (deliberately), I picked up this book again with a degree of trepidation. When I wrote the book, it fully allowed me to process and deal with what had happened to me and allowed my friends and family to understand everything that I did and knew for those many years, without the same questions being asked constantly.

As I had mentioned I had literally cut myself off from almost all my best friends, I couldn't express why and unless I ever felt I was me again had decided not to renew contact. So, people had many questions.

Since finishing the book, I had put the book to one side and not looked at it again until now. Writing this book helped me so much that I honestly felt able to see this as a past experience rather than carry it with me and I needed distance to look at it again.

I actually felt that the book embodied me during those years and so saw this as existing in its own right, something that covered that period for me and would always be there should I need to revisit. By writing this it really helped me close the book literally.

I don't dwell on that period, or the lost years. I am just thankful for every day I have had since I became me again.

It has been an extremely intriguing year and a great deal has happened to me. I have started writing about that. Strangely the experiences of the last several years has helped me in all that has happened.

It turns out as well that this has not been a transitory experience (my mind is once again a trusted companion in all I do) and for that I am forever grateful.

The changes I experienced in my character and the quirks in my memory have in most part stayed with me, although thankfully my humour seems to have returned to my "normal" state.

I welcome those changes like friends, they came into being through necessity but stay with me and already have helped me in so many ways through the last year. The quirks like drinking tea as an example predominantly all stayed with me.

I will be back. I would love to hear any comments and within limits will try to answer any questions you may have. I decided I would answer some questions that people may have had in relation to the book. After some thought, I decided to add this in an appendix, rather than intrude on to the main book.

# Appendix A – Questions and Answers

I have put together, with some help from friends and family some questions that people may want to ask, especially with the benefit of hindsight. The book was written and reflects my thoughts at the time, though surprisingly little has changed in what I think.  I will add readers questions to the next edition of the eBook.

### 1.  Did the changes in the brain ever start again?

No, once they stopped, they never restarted.  I have to say although it was fascinating it was extremely disorientating and I was pleased when things stopped.

### 2.  Did you ever work out how to work with visual basic again?

No, despite looking at things I have created over a period of 15 years, I remember literally nothing about Visual Basic anymore and cannot work out what it does anymore.  I kind of decided it was the brains way of telling me to move on.

### 3.  Do you now drink tea or coffee?

I still drink lots of tea.  I have 4 jars of coffee I have not touched in the last year.  I have no real insight as to why this is the case.

## 4. Did you ever revisit those spreadsheets you so lovingly maintained for years?

I now update 1 of these sheets about once every 2-3 weeks to keep track of my gas/electricity spending, as costs skyrocket. I probably spend 15 minutes a week on it, as opposed to 4-5 hours a day on the complete set. I realise now it was purely something that helped my development and something, somehow, I needed at that time.

## 5. Did your memory gaps reduce at all?

Strangely, I expected this to happen i.e., gradually things that remained missing would fill in. However, that doesn't seem to have happened. I would love to know why.

I also never regained further memories of the earlier years whilst taking anti-psychotics. I don't think I ever will with these.

## 6. Do you still suffer any short-term problems with memory?

My recall of TV shows I watch is much better and I can remember as I watch a TV show what has happened earlier but my memory seems to fade on both films and TV, so I end up rewatching earlier seasons when new seasons come out of TV Shows.

Strangely I don't seem to have short term memory issues with anything other than TV.

## 7. How has your relationship changed with your daughter?

This is something I pick up in my next book. It has developed though this proved far more complex than I had imagined.

## 8. You never mention your diagnosis in the book.  Why is that?

I was diagnosed bi-polar type A.  I have friends that are bi-polar and I see constantly their ups and downs.  Many people have described me as the calmest person they know.  I was unhappy with the diagnosis as I never had mania before in my life or since 2015 and I have never had depression (type A is mania only).

## 9.  You say that what you experienced is brain damage.  Why do you believe that?

I say this because once the mania passed, I found it impossible to think and that remained for years.  I base the brain damage assessment based on what it took to regain function, which was years of repeating the same function and gradual assimilation of knowledge, followed by a rapid growth in cognitive abilities towards the end. In total it took me 6 years to regain full cognitive function.  I can find no other reason that makes sense for the loss and subsequent regaining of cognitive ability.   Basically, I lost cognitive function, it took 6 years to rebuild it.  One way or another that is brain damage.

## 10.  Have you experienced any depression or flashbacks, in the last year since recovery?

I haven't experienced any flashbacks, nightmares, episodes of depression.  I don't really think much about this time other than when discussing the book or updating/editing the book recently.  It surprised me I came out of the whole recovery not resenting the time I lost or angry about it just really just thankful for the recovery and the time I get to be me again, which I never really thought possible.

## 11.  Have there been any signs that the changes may be temporary?

No thankfully not, though I still treat this as a possible outcome.

12. **You mention changes from before you are ill, did any of these prove temporary?**

No, I was actually surprised changes, like being more philosophical about things have stuck with me and show no likelihood of being temporary?

13. **What happened eventually with the friends you reconnected with? Did you manage to stay friends?**

I ended up with a group of 6 friends who I have reconnected with. The duration I knew each at time I disconnected averaged 22 years.

14. **Your dad's friend, who became your friend must have a lot of views about this period having been there throughout?**

I am sure he has. However, he is a stalwart old-fashioned fellow who doesn't like to discuss these sorts of things, he just does them. I asked whether he wanted to talk about these things and he didn't which I completely understand and accept.

15. **What would you say to relatives of people who have suffered brain damage?**

This is the question I need to think about carefully and give full context to my answer so it is a long answer.

I cannot say I am representative of people suffering brain damage as I do not know. The damage I suffered was ot as a result of a blow to the brain that completely damaged beyond repair part of my brain.

For the first two years after this damage occurred, I 100% believe that the medication I was taking inhibited any form of brain recovery. Literally nothing changed. As soon as I stopped taking this medication the recovery started, though from people dealing with me it probably took a year or two before they noticed signs of change at all.

Additionally in the first couple of years whilst on the medication, everyone believed that my cognitive inability was due to the medication. It made sense. It was the only thing that had changed.

It was only when I came off the anti-psychotic medication that people cast the net a little wider.

People didn't really know after that what to do, they knew I may be like that long term (it had been years already) but the effort they expended primarily focused on trying to get me reintegrated with society as I was.

I cannot say that I knew that trying to relearn things would help me and I had very limited capacity when I started trying office tools again specifically Excel. However, I chose it as I had worked with spreadsheets since they first emerged in the second half of the eighties. I had even designed one for an extremely large conglomerate covering hundreds of subsidiaries covering all financial year end accounting. I didn't know when I embarked on this whether it would make any difference at all. When it did, no matter how slowly I just kept going.

Given the above context, what I will say is the following. I feel like my brain repaired itself, I just unlocked some doors that enabled it to do so.

I feel the brain is remarkable and whilst I was effectively locked in my brain to me almost felt like a partner trying to help me and, in some instances, nudge and guide me, especially in the later stages.

What I would say is that the brain is remarkable and from my perspective wants to heal itself if it possibly can. I almost feel like the brain we can't see or touch that we don't access was maybe guiding this process.

I know people told me many times I would never recover, although I feel much more may have been possible if the medical community had been more involved.

To anyone who knows someone who has suffered brain damage, I will say this. Don't give up. See small advances as massive achievements. The vast majority of the effort for me yielded little until suddenly things started to gain traction and movement but that took years. My brain never gave up on me.

During all the time I couldn't express myself Inside I just wanted to be me again, imperfections and all.

**16.  You mention in the later stages, your brain craving interaction. How did this manifest itself?  Do you still believe that?  Are you sure it wasn't you wanting that interaction but maybe not recognising the thoughts?**

This is quite difficult but to me an intriguing one.  In the same way for example you know you are extremely hungry or need to go to the toilet, this manifested at this level.

I would get on and do other things but this "need" would not go away until I had spoken to a few people each day.  It sated when I did this and the need was overpowering.

This only lasted a few weeks but during the conversations I would get waves of memories and parts of my vocabulary back., It would "wash over" me in a sense of all of a sudden, I would have this whole group of things I would know again. I had never experienced anything like it before.

I honestly believe that in this and a few other things I began to see my physical brain/non accessible brain as guiding me, like a big push in the back towards what I had to do to complete my recovery. I still wonder at my brain. Its almost like the part I don't have access to is sentient.

This wasn't me thinking I need to do something, even subconsciously, it was something I had no control over and do nothing to control other than oblige.

## 17. You seem to treat the subject lightly. Almost as though its not serious or are you putting a good show on to cover the hurt?

This is also a tough one. I watched my father carry the pain and the hurt of life's experiences with him every day and his children never were allowed to open the box to discuss it.

I watched so many people go through terrible things and wondered how on earth they could do it, be so brave, live with such adversity.

So, if someone asked me before this happened how I would feel after it happened, I would imagine so much hurt and pain.

My reality was actually different. For years I couldn't literally feel sorry for myself even if I wanted to. I didn't have the cognitive power to think about it. It is so hard to describe.

Somehow, I knew I existed. I saw things but they passed through me without registering. Some things in those stages I only recognised years later (some somehow must have been stored) though so much was just lost.

Once I stopped the drugs and started doing things again and again on the computer, I was doing something, active and just initially did what I knew I had previously known even though I couldn't remember.

Back to the original question, there was sadness for example when I saw the hugs between my wife and daughter and couldn't express how much I missed that or a kiss from my wife as the years went by, I am sure they seemed pointless.

There were also periods where I felt useless (I was) and a burden (I was). Its only now while typing this I feel tinges of sadness about it.

However, when writing the book, I felt I should recognise those emotions but just be completely honest about what was happening.

For me this allowed me to perform what I have called a cathartic exorcism of everything I experienced. I recognised it and let it go. It never came back.

As to the tone it really is how I feel about it all. Weirdly given it has happened, I believe it has shaped me a little in a positive way and in a way, I am glad that happened before I died as I believe it has changed my view of life and death.

I am more accepting of life, much more conscious of what I want to do in my life and more importantly not do, I was always positive but feel even more positive. I feel I know more about what I am capable of from a life experience perspective.

# Appendix B - 2015 writings whilst manic

This makes me cringe but it's an important part of my story. I mentioned in this doc that I started writing stuff, while going through a mental breakdown. I have a ton of this stuff, should anyone want to see it.

What surprises me most is every now and again someone buys it on Amazon (you can't take these down once published, I think to ensure past purchases remain honoured in future).

I feel like writing an apology each time. I can only be thankful it wasn't my real name. Selecting excerpts is going to be painful for me but I need to do it, so here goes.

## An Ode to President Obama - A good man

Well, they can't talk about your presidency without saying
Obama care......d
You did though, in every worry line
In every grimace to atrocities
In your eloquence that was lost to sheer volume of work
Why is it so difficult to take something that matters and make it right?
If the most powerful man in the world can't
No wonder others also turn grey

You cared, you tried and for that I for one am thankful you were there
Once this passes your articulate considered speeches will return
And once again they will touch me

I would vote for you for a third term
And I am British and can't vote
Doesn't matter though
It's the thought that counts.
Really it is


I like Obama, I really do. Yes, I know there are no third terms. I just reproduced what was said at the time. I suppose it's not complete drivel. He is in my mind one of the greatest former presidents and I suppose you cannot openly see the hand of mania on this (though it is there and I can sense it). Not exactly a literary review but I never promised that.

## An ode to Kermode

Yes, I say, not an ode to a commode
The TV Film Critic
No BS, No Banter
Want to know, Is it Good?
Want a chat, please go elsewhere
Want someone to trust
Someone like Roger Ebert, whose every sentence meant something
Mark Kermode understands
Communication, Clarity, Concise, Precise and if I am allowed
Brevity
Or is that tortuous!

This is about Mark Kermode, who is the BBC film critic. He is an excellent critic and I have always rated him. The title shows my brain waves. My literary comment. Not as batshit as some of my other stuff.

## Ms J.K. Rowling

My Daughter adores your books
I read them all myself
An 8-year-old reading several hundred pages is immersed in dragons,
and wizards and magic and mystery
You created all that
You recreated the British Film Industry and made our actors front
and centre globally
You did all of that
You helped create an amazing theme park and further details of that
world
However, my daughter slept with dreams of Magic for nearly a year
And for that I thank you.


OK everyone knows and most have read JK Rowling.  Her books
were great and I enjoyed them as much as my daughter. About the
Ode.  A bit of a cringe fest and it's just some sentences slapped on the
page.  Doesn't even attempt to be a form of poetry.  My assessment.
I'm sorry I subjected you to this.

**An Ode to Bill Turnbull**

Strictly that wasn't dancing
But you knew that
Bill, you know we love you
We could cuddle you
You seem like the nicest guy on the planet
On TV at breakfast
I have just a few questions now you are in Manchester Bill
What's on TV when you eat your breakfast?
Where do you sit on the sofa at home (on the Right perhaps?)
Do you cross your knee when watching the TV?
Love you to bits Bill
My Favourite ever Breakfast TV presenter


Bill Turnbull. He was both my and my wife's favourite ever breakfast presenter and in the scheme of things still is. I'm holding on to my seat in pain at the early parts but actually I would be kind of interested to know the answers to the last 3 questions. My assessment, should have skipped the ode and given the questions to BBC Newsround for some clever 9-year-old to ask.

## From the partially completed books (written whilst Manic)

Right, this is the bit I have been avoiding, since I started this book. I am not going to search for the most messed up bit, so there may well be worse. This is the mental equivalent of me stepping into a challenge on I'm a celebrity. I will never be ready for this. Hang tight. The first is from my "book" about the experience of a meltdown.

I need to give some clarification. At this point I thought I was the cleverest of them all, with insights no-one else had. I know, right. Anyway my "plan" was to write a novel that melded Catch-22 with To Kill a Mockingbird.

From those who read Catch-22 the main character finds himself in what is termed a Catch-22. In order to leave the army, you must be mad, but to leave the army during a war you are displaying the logic of not wanting to get killed so you can't be mad. Throughout the book everyone laughs at the main character (yep, me too). However, at the end, the book pivots and makes you realise you were the idiot not the character. Joseph Heller is my favourite author. He can do didactic like no one else.

Anyway, the point was in my book, I wanted people to laugh at the main character, all the way through and then right at the end to make them realise the main character was actually sane all the way through.

I don't think anyone who has read To Kill a Mockingbird, can ever, ever forget the line at the end where Atticus Finch describes the horrors of what happened to that poor little girl in the book.

That line. I am glad this is a book not me having to say it as I would blubber it. He had told the jury to close their eyes before the story and his final line was "Now imagine she was white".

So, my idea was to meld the two books and do some kind of speech where right at the end I say "and now imagine this story had happened to you". Again, not a bad idea. Actually, I have to have a grudging respect. I would have liked to have thought of that. Well, I know I did, but not a sane version of me.

I think probably that's why a publisher engaged with me. Derivative but a mix of two books. So basically, I stole and mixed an idea from two books not one. However, to be fair to me, I love both of those books. So, all of that information now in play (the world's longest introduction). Get ready for some batshit execution.

My worries were the changes in my health and the fact that my aunt wouldn't stop bouncing meaning I couldn't sleep at night, only having 15 or so hours sleep in 8 nights. This would prove crucial in the next 48 hours.

Over the next 2 days I only slept 1 hour. I started practicing for the weekend when I knew I'd be alone, started sending emails to all those around me. Knowing I wouldn't get a response I would target the emails and they were self-fulfilling. Each led on to the next, and the next.

They got darker, and darker and more and more frequent and then, I slept.

I awoke to a mess. I had had (yes two hads, now three) a bit of a break. I had sent some pretty messed up mails to all my bosses including the owner of the company. The mails were pretty strange lots of swearing, and unlike me. Must have been the Imodium I thought.

The mails though were a little disturbing dark, vitriolic, nasty stuff. Wow lay off the Imodium super drug I thought.

I had also and unknowingly sent each mail through to every LinkedIn contact I had ever made, which was nearly 700. In one night, I had destroyed my career, but that's another book. Ho Hum, so luckily, they had banned me after 24 hours. Never thought I would say that.

I am not exactly sure where in the timing of things this was written. My state deteriorated quickly and this is after the breakdown, so close to hospitalisation (I think). At first glance it just appears odd, but it's sending my spider sense tingling.

There are loads of little red flags. Mainly, it's just not the way you would say something. I feel a little sick looking at it. Maybe it's just me and what I associate with at that time. I know I was in warped clarity mode.

That wasn't much of an extract. Like the bushtucker trials or whatever they are called on I'm a celebrity (I don't watch it). I just went in and out as quick as I could. However, I have done it once so (deep breaths) will try again for some more messed up extracts from the same insane ramblings.

Many friends came to visit that day as I balanced slushies against normal service. Billy No mates with bloo seemed like the worst option. I waited for normal service and ate more. Normal service didn't resume for another 24 hours.

If you have ever seen Pooh bear (oh yes, I do mean Pooh bear), leaning over the honey pot, looking at the honey, you basically have what I was doing for the next 24 hours. However, I wasn't seeing honey.

Sometimes you make friends that won't be forever. Mine were not forever, but it would be fair to say, there were no closer friends for the next 24 hours.

I mentioned before I was heavy set (now there's a nice way of saying it). I would have considered my exercise to be getting up, getting in the car and driving to work. However rather forcibly, every hour I ran up and down stairs. I felt proud when I wrote to people, I had done 30 stair laps in a day. However, if I hadn't, bloo would have made a mess of the carpet, that white wine wouldn't clear.

So, 24 hours passed, and I passed 24 hours' worth of bloo. Sleep you ask, now that is a very good question. If at this stage you patting yourself on the back, stop. It was me who asked the question; you do know that right? Given the circumstances of the book I have to check. Several thousand of these questions are asked later of me. "Do you hear voices from the TV?". I knew that one "Only when it's switched on". You have to be so careful! Hello, wait a second my plug socket is calling me.

No, it wasn't, I was kidding. However, if they do call you, you need to tell someone. Really. I am not kidding. My own spiral into an event was pretty darn good. I have asked Susan if I could get a recommendation or a badge or something. Susan did think that a bit silly. Later I realised humour can get you into trouble! Not with Susan.

When I said to Susan that everyone is looking at me as the mad uncle on the dance floor, wondering whether to claim me and whether he is "nuts forever", Susan said we will claim you as our mad uncle. Anyone touches Susan in this and gloves are off.

I don't wear gloves. Now I have a dilemma. What would I do if you took me up on this? Now see what you made me do. I will pop out to Woolworths (Listen guys I know it's not there anymore) and buy some just in case.

Wow this bit is not so enjoyable. At first glance this may seem quirky and fun. It's not, its batshit with early signs of madness. My skin creeps when I read this.

I am probably meant to come to terms with who I was (sounds like the sort of thing a psychiatrist would say... a bit bollocks but thought out). To that I say I can't and I won't. I sound petulant. I don't like that person and never will.

# Appendix C – My Background

However, I look at this next bit, it appears to be bragging and if it wasn't needed to give context to the fact that I needed my brain in my life, I would delete. It is the sort of stuff people I hate do in that they unnecessarily tell you their good deeds and achievements, when all you asked them for was a bar of chocolate.

Please believe me when I say this hurts me more saying it, than it does you reading it. It makes me retch a bit. Try not to hate me. Sorry.

In my work: -

- I created a spreadsheet system for the largest subsidiary of a mult national consumer goods company covering over 200 companies, to manage their accounting before Spreadsheets existed in my first job.
- I devised the first system for remote supply of information to a stock exchange (which was worth 7% of entire turnover of the Stock exchange at the time)
- I was selected in the UK as the only client to meet the inventor of the operating system the vast majority of the city was using at the age of 24.
- I was responsible for the first major program in the whole of the Bank to move the entire trading platforms from mainframes to Unix, through all stages (the mainframe took up 1100 square feet)

- I spent 10 years contracting after this working on the largest project in Europe at an Exchange, on getting trains running between the UK and France, dealing with the largest program ever attempted by a major pension fund and at the end being the person responsible to the CEO for putting that system live after several years of work costing many tens of millions of pounds.
- After this I spent 15 years in high end consulting dealing with C level professionals including CEO's, CTO's etc. I spent over a decade as one of my functions being responsible for the strategic units of the consultancies I worked at.
- As part of that I oversaw and conducted myself reviews of companies in a 2-week period, to analyse an internal issue that they themselves couldn't solve. These tended to be massive challenges that involved me often several hundred documents and interviewing the whole of the senior management structure to work out what was going wrong and to suggest how to fix it, all within a 2-week period. Most of my recommendations were implemented.
- These studies I personally conducted were over 40 and included the global supply chain of the top UK supermarket chain, the entire running of the UK blood service, The entire running of a TV channel from Acquisition to Broadcast, the rollout mechanism for one of the world's leading Mass Spectrometry divisions, The running of Credit Rate Derivates in a global bank (had Russian ex space scientists working on Quants) and many others of similar ilk.
- I have worked with leaders in their field throughout this with many systems I worked on being ground-breaking. I worked with for example the team leader who invented the Rank Xerox Star Workstation which was the foundation for both windows and MacOS.

- I worked with the inventor of multi-processor architecture that form the basis of all computer chips today. I conducted reviews in research labs like a telecoms company the US East coast analysing the team, whose job it was to analyse everything that went through the internet on their infrastructure (think 5 times BT), which required a Cray Supercomputer costing many tens of millions of pounds). In short, I needed my brain.

Printed in Great Britain
by Amazon

16443324R00088